POPE AMONGST
THE SATIRISTS 1660–1750

ALEXANDER POPE

POPE AMONGST THE SATIRISTS

1660–1750

Brean Hammond

NORTHCOTE
BRITISH COUNCIL

© Copyright 2005 by Brean Hammond

First published in 2005 by Northcote House Publishers Ltd, Horndon, Tavistock, Devon, PL19 9NQ, United Kingdom.
Tel: +44 (01822) 810066. Fax: +44 (01822) 810034.

British Library Cataloguing-in-Publication Data
A catalogue record for this book is available from the British Library

ISBN 0-7463-1083-8 hardcover
ISBN 0-7463-0823-X paperback

Typeset by TW Typesetting, Plymouth, Devon
Printed and bound in the United Kingdom by
Athenaeum Press Ltd., Gateshead, Tyne & Wear

Contents

Chronological Outline, 1660–1744

This chronology outlines some of the main historical events of a period spanning the Restoration of King Charles II in 1660 and the death of Alexander Pope in 1744. It lists dates of publication of the major works discussed in the text (dates for plays are of first performance), dates of birth and other information about the most important writers born in the period, and the main events in the life of Alexander Pope, who is the book's central figure.

1660   General Monk pilots return of Charles II to English throne after restored Rump Parliament has forced abdication of Richard Cromwell. Declaration of Breda promises lawful parliamentary settlement. 8 May: Convention Parliament invites Charles to be restored as monarch. 29 May: Charles returns to London. Theatres given permission to reopen. Foundation of Royal Society.

1661   Charles' first Parliament establishes the Anglican Church and enacts a series of repressive measures, the Clarendon Code: e.g. the Act of Uniformity, requiring clergy to be ordained by bishops and use only the Book of Common Prayer.

1663   First theatre opens in Drury Lane. Samuel Butler, *Hudibras*, Part I (Part II published in 1664).

1664   New Jersey founded. Vanbrugh born. Religious meetings outside church penalized. Etherege's first play, *The Comical Revenge*.

1665   Newton conceives idea of gravitation and Hooke discovers living cells in plants. Second Dutch War begins. 7 June: first incidence of plague reported in London.

1666   France joins Dutch and war goes badly for Charles. Great Fire breaks out in a bakehouse in Pudding Lane. St Paul's and much of central London destroyed. Covenanters crushed at Battle of Pentland Hills.

1667   Treaty of Breda concludes Second Dutch War after a Dutch fleet enters the Medway and captures English flagship *Royal Charles*. Milton, *Paradise Lost*. Birth of Swift.

1668   Newton builds first reflecting telescope. Dryden, *Essay of Dramatick Poesy*.

1670   King concludes an open and a secret Treaty of Dover with Louis XIV, in the latter of which he agrees to convert to Catholicism and restore it to England. Congreve born. Rebuilding of London churches under Wren. Carolinas founded.

1671   Plays by Shadwell, Behn, and Wycherley performed. Dryden, *Marriage à la Mode*. Milton, *Paradise Regained* and *Samson Agonistes*. Rochester, *The Rehearsal*.

1672   Charles issues controversial Declaration of Indulgence, permitting freedom of worship and assuming right to cancel all penal legislation against Catholics and Protestants. Third Anglo-Dutch war begins because Charles pledges support for Louis XIV against Dutch. Newton presents research on light and optics to Royal Society.

1673   Test Act deprives Catholics and nonconformists of public office.

1674   Third Dutch War ends. New Amsterdam becomes New York. Death of Milton. Opening of rebuilt Drury Lane Theatre. Widespread concern that James, Duke of York, is a Catholic. Moves made to exclude him from the succession.

1675   Wycherley's *The Country Wife* performed. Court painter Lely paints Nell Gwyn. Work on new St Paul's begins. Rochester producing poems in manuscript for limited circulation.

1676 Walpole born. Wycherley, *Plain Dealer*; Etherege, *Man of Mode*.

1677 Dryden, *All for Love*; Behn, *The Rover*.

1678 So-called Popish Plot to assassinate the King whipped up by Titus Oates and Israel Tonge. Disabling Act debars Catholics from sitting in Parliament. Lord Treasurer Danby supports the Plot but is later dismissed from office. Bunyan, *Pilgrim's Progress*.

1679 Duke of Monmouth wins victories against Scottish Covenanters rebelling against repressive measures. Bill of Exclusion prepared against Duke of York.

1680 Shaftesbury organizes nationwide petitions to exclude Duke of York from the throne. Petitioners become known as 'Whigs' and opponents are Tories. Death of Rochester. Purcell, *Dido and Aeneas*. Otway, *The Orphan* and *The Soldier's Fortune*.

1681 Test Act (1673) requires all Crown officials including MPs to swear oath of allegiance to the Crown and receive Church of England communion at least once a year. Its enforcement prompts eighty bishops to resign. Charles rejects Exclusion Bill and dissolves Parliament. Dryden, *Absalom and Achitophel*.

1682 Halley's comet observed. Dryden, *MacFlecknoe*; Otway, *Venice Preserv'd*.

1683 Discovery of Rye House Plot to assassinate Charles. Execution of Algernon Sidney and Lord William Russell. Ashmolean Museum opens in Oxford.

1685 2 Feb.: death of Charles II. James II succeeds. Duke of Monmouth lands at Lyme Regis to contest Crown. 6 July: crushed at Sedgemoor. Supporters harshly sentenced by Judge Jeffreys at 'Bloody Assizes'.

1686 Catholics readmitted by James II to army.

1687 James expels Fellows of Magdalen, Oxford, for refusing to appoint a Catholic, Dr Parker, as President. Declares liberty of conscience in a Declaration, widely seen as pro-Catholic. Dryden's *Hind and the Panther* defends his conversion. Newton, *Principia Mathematica*.

1688 James requires Second Declaration of Liberty of Conscience to be read in churches. Archbishop Sancroft refuses, and the Seven Bishops are acquitted of treason charges. A son, James Stuart, is born to King James but widely suspected to be illegitimate. This triggers off Glorious Revolution. William of Orange invited to take the English throne. 5 Nov.: William lands at Torbay. Dec.: James flees to France. Behn, *Oroonoko*. Alexander Pope born.

1689   Convention Parliament declares James's abdication. Joint rule offered to William and Mary. Declaration of Rights bolsters parliamentary power at expense of the monarch. James contests situation in Ireland. Tyrconnel supports him, while Protestants in Northern Ireland declare for William, who is taking refuge in Derry. Derry besieged by a Catholic army. Toleration Act establishes permanent freedom of worship, and Bill of Rights enacts the liberties established in 1688, guaranteeing Protestant succession. Britain at war with France, and Highland Jacobite rebellion under Bonnie Dundee is successful at Killiecrankie but peters out. Swift becomes Secretary to Sir William Temple at Moor Park and meets Esther Johnson (Stella).

1690   Archbishop Sancroft at the head of those (non-jurors) who will not swear allegiance to William. Large-scale purges. William defeats James's army at the Boyne. Locke, *Two Treatises of Government* and *Essay Concerning Human Understanding*.

1691   William 'pacifies' Ireland. James surrenders under Treaty of Limerick and goes to France. Purcell and Dryden collaborate on operatic *King Arthur*. Thomas Southerne, *The Wives Excuse*.

1692   Macdonald of Glencoe is massacred by Campbells on the pretext of failing to swear oath to William.

1693   Commencement of the National Debt, when William borrows £1 million at 10 per cent to finance French wars. Beginning of 'financial revolution'. First plays of Congreve. Locke, *Ideas on Education*.

1694   Foundation of Bank of England for government financial services. Death of Queen Mary.

1695   Foundation of Bank of Scotland. Death of Purcell. Congreve, *Love for Love*. Southerne's dramatic version of *Oroonoko*.

1696   Plot to assassinate William III discovered. Pope at school in a Catholic seminary at Twyford, Hants. Vanbrugh, *The Relapse*.

1697   War against France ends in Treaty of Ryswick. Hogarth born. Vanbrugh, *The Provoked Wife*.

1698   Slave trade officially sanctioned. London Stock Exchange founded. White's chocolate house becomes Tory HQ. Jeremy Collier publishes *A Short View . . .*, a powerful attack on the English stage for immorality.

1699   Scottish trading colony on Darien (Panama) is a disastrous failure, owing to lack of support from East India Company. Farquhar's debut as playwright. Dampier explores western coast of Australia.

1700   Death of Dryden. English throne to pass to Electress Sophia of Hanover on death of Princess [Queen] Anne's last surviving child – ratified 1701 in Act of Settlement. Vanbrugh begins Castle Howard. Congreve, *Way of the World*. Pope's family moves to Binfield in Windsor Forest.

1702   Death of William III. Queen Anne succeeds. First English daily newspaper, *Daily Courant*. John Churchill (Duke of Marlborough) captain-general of British forces.

1703   Defoe is sentenced to the pillory for writing an ironic attack on Dissenters (Protestants who did not accept the Church of England). Marlborough winning European battles against France. Methuen Treaty starts the British importing of port from Portugal. Rowe's first 'she-tragedy', *The Fair Penitent*.

1704   Alexander Selkirk marooned on Juan Fernandez (original of *Robinson Crusoe*). Battle of Blenheim. Swift, *A Tale of a Tub* and *The Battle of the Books*.

1705   Funds to build Blenheim Palace gifted to Marlborough by grateful nation. Vanbrugh commences building. Vanbrugh opens Queen's Haymarket, dedicated to opera.

1706   Thomas Twining begins major tea-importing business from Tom's coffee house. Victory for the British, Dutch, and Danish alliance at Ramillies begins the dismantling of Spanish Empire and paves the way for

British trade and slaving monopolies. Farquhar, *The Recruiting Officer*.

1707   1 May: Act of Union between England and Scotland. Uniting of Parliaments at Westminster. Sixteen Scottish Lords and forty-five MPs. Union Jack combines St George and St Andrew crosses. Farquhar, *The Beaux Stratagem*. Birth of Fielding.

1708   Newcomen patents steam engine for pumping water out of mines. United East India Company begins its influential exploitation of India. The 'Old Pretender', son of James II, lands in Scotland but is repulsed.

1709   Abraham Darby produces high-quality, low-cost iron in Coalbrookdale, Salop. Steele's *Tatler* is the first of a new generation of literary periodicals. Pope, *Pastorals*.

1710   Henry Sacheverell, a hot-headed High Church Tory is impeached but gains massive popular support. Handel comes to Britain and his opera *Rinaldo* is premiered. Congreve, *Collected Works*, in 3 vols.

1711   Pope, *An Essay on Criticism*. Friendship with Addison and Steele, who begin composing *The Spectator*. Shaftesbury, *Characteristics of Men, Manners, Opinions and Times*.

1712   Two-canto version of Pope, *The Rape of the Lock*. Pope acquainted with Scriblerians Swift, Gay, Arbuthnot, Parnell. Oxford attends Scriblerian meetings. Arbuthnot, *History of John Bull*.

1713   Pope, *Windsor Forest*. Swift becomes Dean of St Patrick's Cathedral, Dublin. Peace of Utrecht between France and Britain. Meetings of Scriblerians begin.

1714   Five-canto *The Rape of the Lock*. Death of Queen Anne. Accession of George I. Whig ministry formed under Townshend, including Walpole. End of meetings of Scriblerus Club. Swift to Ireland. Nicholas Rowe, *Jane Shore*.

1715   Pope, *The Temple of Fame* and *Iliad* I. Befriends Lady Mary Wortley Montagu. Oxford and Bolingbroke impeached. Jacobite Rebellion in support of 'Old Pretender' ended in defeats at Preston and Sheriffmuir. Bolingbroke to France; Oxford imprisoned. Walpole rises to Chancellor of Exchequer.

1716   Pope, *Iliad* II. Family moves to Chiswick. Gay, *Trivia*.
1717   Pope, *Iliad* III. First volume of Pope's *Works*. Death of
        Pope's father. *Three Hours after Marriage* by Pope, Gay,
        and Arbuthnot may be mocking Susanna Centlivre,
        prolific playwright. Certainly mocks critic John
        Dennis, adversary of Pope.
1718   Pope, *Iliad* IV. Death of Parnell. Susanna Centlivre, *A
        Bold Stroke for a Wife*. England declares war on Spain.
1719   Pope and his mother to Twickenham. Defoe, *Robinson
        Crusoe*, and Eliza Haywood, *Love in Excess*, contend
        for emerging novel readership.
1720   Pope, *Iliad* V, VI. South Sea Bubble fiasco, after the
        company offers to take over the National Debt,
        leading to ruinous financial speculation. Birth of
        Prince Charles Edward Stuart, the Young Pretender.
1721   Pope edits Parnell's poems and begins work on
        Shakespeare edition. Walpole appointed First Lord of
        Treasury. Lady Mary Wortley Montagu introduces
        smallpox inoculation, taken up by Princess of Wales.
1722   Pope collaborates with Fenton and Broome on *Odys-
        sey* edition. Bishop Atterbury charged with a Jacobite
        plot. Walpole comes to power as head of government.
        Marlborough dies. Defoe, *Moll Flanders*.
1723   Pope brings out edition of Buckingham's *Works*.
        Suspected of Jacobite sympathies and appears as
        witness at Atterbury's trial. Atterbury convicted and
        exiled. Bolingbroke returns to England briefly. John
        Thurmond produces *Harlequin Dr Faustus*, a panto-
        mime, at Drury Lane – later to be mocked by Pope in
        The Dunciad.
1724   Swift earns reputation as Irish patriot for *Drapier's
        Letters*, written to oppose William Wood's patent to
        debase Irish copper coinage. Defoe, *Roxana*. Notorious
        highwayman Jack Sheppard is executed – possible
        prototype for Gay's Macheath in *The Beggar's Opera*.
1725   Pope, six-volume edition of Shakespeare, and *Odyssey*
        I–III. Bolingbroke settles at Dawley Farm, near neigh-
        bour to Pope.
1726   Pope, *Odyssey* IV–V. Swift, *Gulliver's Travels*.
        Theobald attacks Pope in *Shakespeare Restored*. Boling-

broke commences anti-government *Craftsman* essays. Pope and Swift together for a period. Thomson, *Seasons*, begins to appear.

1727 Pope–Swift, *Miscellanies* I–II. George I dies and George II accedes. War between England and Spain. Death of Isaac Newton. Gay, *Fables*.

1728 Pope–Swift, *Miscellanies* III, includes *Peri Bathous*. Three-book *Dunciad* appears with Theobald as hero. Gay, *The Beggar's Opera*. Fielding's first play, *Love in Several Masques*.

1729 Larger edition of *Dunciad* with key and commentaries, *The Dunciad Variorum*. Swift, *A Modest Proposal*. Gay's sequel to *The Beggar's Opera*, *Polly* is banned.

1730 Fielding, *The Author's Farce* mocks, among others, Thomson's *Sophonisba*. Fielding, *Tom Thumb the Great*.

1731 Pope, *Epistle to Burlington*, controversial due to portrait of 'Timon' being taken by Duke of Chandos as a personal attack.

1732 Pope–Swift, *Miscellanies* IV. Gay dies. Opening of Covent Garden Theatre in London.

1733 Pope, *Epistle to Bathurst*, *Imit. Hor. Sat. II.i*, and *Essay on Man* I–III. Pope's mother dies. Walpole's Excise Scheme defeated. Committed political opposition to Walpole spearheaded by Bolingbroke's *Craftsman*.

1734 Pope, *Epistle to Cobham*, *Essay on Man* IV, and *Imit. Hor. Sat. II.ii*. Fielding, *Don Quixote in England*. Theobald's seven-volume edition of Shakespeare appears.

1735 Pope, *Epistle to Dr Arbuthnot* and *Epistle to a Lady*; second vol. of Pope's *Works*. Scandalous publisher Edmund Curll prints pirated copy of Pope's letters. Arbuthnot dies. Bolingbroke returns to France. Swift, *Works*, published in Dublin.

1736 Fielding, *Pasquin*. Harrison invents chronometer. Porteous Riots in Edinburgh.

1737 Pope, *Imit. Hor. Sat. II.ii* and *Epistle II.i*. Authorized edition of Pope's letters is controversial. *Essay on Man* attacked by Swiss theologian Crousaz. Queen Caroline dies. Prince of Wales quarrels with his father and retires from Court to lead 'patriot' opposition to

Walpole's Whig government. Passing of Theatrical Licensing Act, partly in response to Fielding's *The Historical Register for the Year 1736*, restricts playhouses to two (Drury Lane and Covent Garden) and imposes censorship. Fielding commences study of law. Samuel Johnson and David Garrick set out from Lichfield to London.

1738   Pope, *Imit. Hor. Sat. I.vi, Epistle I.i*, and *Epilogue to the Satires*. Pope entertains Bolingbroke at Twickenham. Samuel Johnson, *London*, is seen to be a 'patriot' poem. John Wesley commences Methodist revival in England.

1739   Pope winters with Ralph Allen, patron of Fielding and inspiration behind Squire Allworthy in *Tom Jones*, at Prior Park near Bath. Warburton defends Pope from Crousaz. War of Jenkins' Ear breaks out between England and Spain. Hume, *Treatise on Human Nature*. Swift, *Verses on the Death of Dr Swift*.

1740   Cibber publishes his autobiography, *Apology for the Life of Colley Cibber*. Samuel Richardson, *Pamela*. Arne and Thomson collaborate on 'Rule Britannia'.

1741   Pope brings out *Memoirs of Martinus Scriblerus*. Richardson and Cibber both mocked in Fielding's *Shamela*. David Garrick makes his acting debut and gives his famous performance as Richard III.

1742   A fourth book of *The Dunciad* is published as *The New Dunciad*. Walpole retires from politics. Fielding, *Joseph Andrews*. Swift declared of 'unsound mind', perhaps the result of a chronic disease now known as Ménière's syndrome. Handel, *Messiah*, performed in Dublin. Edward Young, *Night Thoughts*.

1743   Complete revision of *The Dunciad, in Four Books*, with Cibber as hero. Fielding publishes *Miscellanies*, *Jonathan Wild*, and *A Journey from This World to the Next*.

1744   30 May: Pope dies at Twickenham. France at war with England. Johnson, *Life of Savage*. John Newbery publishes *A Little Pretty Pocket-Book* for children.

1745   19 Oct.: death of Swift. Landing of the Young Pretender in Scotland; advances to Derby by December.

Abbreviations

B.   Alexander Pope, *Peri Bathous; or, The Art of Sinking in Poetry*, quoted from *The Prose Works of Alexander Pope*, ii. *1725–1744*, ed. Rosemary Cowler (Oxford, 1986)

D.   *The Works of John Dryden*, ed. Edward Niles Hooker, H. T. Swedenberg, et al. (Berkeley and Los Angeles, 1955–)

M.   Alexander Pope et al., *Memoirs of the Extraordinary Life, Works, and Discoveries of Martinus Scriblerus*, ed. Charles Kerby-Miller (Oxford, 1950; repr.1988)

R.   *The Works of John Wilmot, Earl of Rochester*, ed. Harold Love (Oxford, 1999)

P.   *The Poems of Alexander Pope*, ed. John Butt (London, 1963; repr. 1989)

S.   *The Prose Works of Jonathan Swift*, ed. Herbert Davis et al., 14 vols. (Oxford, 1939–68)

Introduction

The period 1660–1750 has a fair claim to being called the Golden Age of satire written in the English language, because many of the most enduring works written during this era were satirical. Why did satire achieve such prominence? In the early phase of the English Civil War, unprecedented freedom of expression was achieved, even if the end to all censorship as advocated by John Milton in *Areopagitica* never was. That freedom was not widely used, however, for the purpose of exposing individuals or institutions to ridicule. Men and women of the Civil War were earnest in what they had to say. Religious and political debates required high seriousness; humour was a wasteful frivolity. After the Restoration of King Charles II in 1660, relative freedom of expression was sanctioned as part of the monarch's 'easy' image, in reaction to the austerity of the Cromwellian era. It did not extend far beyond Court circles, but within the epicurean, atheistical fraternities of aristocratic rakes, wit was highly regarded and astonishing familiarities could be taken if they were taken wittily. The Puritans of the earlier era were naturally fair game. The first important satire of the Restoration was Samuel Butler's *Hudibras*, published in two parts in 1663 and 1664. Hudibras is a modern-day knight errant, who sets out on horseback to avenge insults to the Christian religion. The first part of the poem is entirely spent in breaking up a bear baiting that Hudibras is convinced will destroy the Protestant reformation if it is allowed to go on, the target here being the extremism of the Puritan crusade against pleasure and popular entertainment. Butler was a pioneer in the use of the burlesque and mock-heroic techniques that would be taken to a high level of refinement in the work of Pope. Hudibras's fight with Talgol the Butcher is described in terms of a combat between epic heroes, complete with divine intervention, rather than as the street brawl that it is. And the informal octosyllabic metre, deploying outlandishly comic rhymes and releasing obscene connotations, would be developed later in the comic verse of Swift:

> This said, with hasty rage he snatch'd
> His Gun-shot, that in holsters watch'd;
> And bending Cock, he level'd full
> Against th'outside of *Talgol*'s Skull;
> Vowing that he should ne're stir further,
> Nor henceforth Cow or Bullock murther.
> But *Pallas* came in shape of Rust,
> And 'twixt the Spring and Hammer thrust
> Her *Gorgon*-shield, which made the Cock
> Stand stiff as if 'twere turn'd t'a stock.
> Meanwhile fierce *Talgol* gath'ring might,
> With rugged Truncheon charg'd the *Knight*.
> And he his rusty Pistol held
> To take the blow on, like a Shield .
> .   .   .   .
> But when his nut-brown Sword was out,
> Couragiously he laid about,
> Imprinting many a wound upon
> His mortal foe the Truncheon.[1]

Puritans remained a target for satirists in the Carolean period. In the most successful play by the Royalist Aphra Behn, *The Rover* (1677), the main comic butt is a tight-fisted and provincial country gentleman called Blunt, who is on the Parliamentary side in the Civil War. Lucetta persuades him that she will grant her sexual favours (without charge), but, groping towards her bed in shirt and drawers, Blunt is let down by a trapdoor into a common sewer, from which he emerges on all fours a minute or two later with the evidence of his humiliation on his face and body.

Such raw-boned attacks on those who were outside the Church of England (there was just as much anti-Catholic as anti-Puritan satire) were not, however, the main achievements of the period's satirical writing. Satire's mission would be to

2

make itself into an art form – to transcend the boundary of mere name calling that earlier Elizabethan satirists such as John Marston and Joseph Hall took it to be. Central to that civilizing mission is John Dryden, and it is in these terms that his art is understood in Chapter 1. But what were the conditions that paved the way for the transformation of satire into an acceptable artistic form?

After the 'Revolution' of 1688, the various acts passed to enable a smoother and more equitable working relationship between King and Parliament created the root conditions for the flourishing of poetic satire that was not exclusively coterie based and circulated in manuscript. Greater freedom of speech resulted from the forging of a more democratic (though of course not by modern standards *actually* democratic) society, one that had to take public opinion more into account. Developing the pioneering work of Jürgen Habermas, historians and cultural critics have commented on the emergence of a 'public sphere', discourses created by and for new forms of public space such as coffee houses, museums and galleries, and circulating libraries, where opinions could be canvassed that were not licensed by the official agencies of Court, Church, and State.[2] The last years of Stuart reign had created divisions in English society that echoed those of the Civil War. Factions were created out of those who insisted that a rightful monarch could not be deposed and those who considered that he could if he failed to observe the fundamental terms of the English constitution. Such factions would in the decades to come achieve respectability as legitimately differing political parties; and vast amounts of satirical writing would be generated by the desire, first to drive one's political opponents into extinction, and later merely to render them absurd as society grew more tolerant and began to understand the importance of institutionalized parliamentary opposition. In the absence of other sources of news, public events were commented upon in satirical broadsheets hawked about the streets or provided in coffee houses. Manuscript poems were eagerly collected and bound into volumes. A modern seven-volume edition of such material is available under the title *Poems on Affairs of State*; and a brief glance at this monumental work shows how the Popish Plot and the Exclusion Crisis of 1677–81, the trial and death of

3

the Earl of Shaftesbury, Monmouth's rebellion, the trial of the Seven Bishops, the birth of James II's son, the Williamite wars and the Act of Union between England and Scotland – indeed, all the salient political events of the period 1680–1710 – gave rise to poems, prose treatises, and pamphlets the object of which was to ridicule one's political enemies and boost one's own partisan point of view.[3]

But the increased toleration created by the Revolution Settlement had effects more complex than simply the vacation of a space in which writers could express themselves satirically about politics. When in 1695 the Licensing Act was permitted to lapse, even if by governmental oversight rather than by any intention to relax the laws on expression, and when in the early years of the eighteenth century a copyright act was passed that for the first time protected literary property, a very considerable impetus was given to the emerging literary and journalistic professions. Those men and women of the 'middling sort' who came to regard writing for a living as a possible and legitimate career aspiration did not usually find satire a congenial mode of expression. Writers of a predominantly Whiggish persuasion, such as Daniel Defoe (who could be devastatingly satirical on occasion), Richard Blackmore, Richard Steele, Joseph Addison, John Dennis, and Nicholas Rowe, on the whole distrusted wit and satire. It was not kind, it was not humane, it was ungenerous; it was elitist because it relied on there being people who were its victims or who did not get the joke. Perhaps unaware of the extent of the paradox, Sir Richard Blackmore published in 1699 a poetic *Satire against Wit*. Blackmore need not have worried that his poem would be contaminated by that quality. Earnestly afraid of the agility and idleness of the wits, positing a tie-up between wit and immorality, the poem shows us what happens to satire when it fails to invent comic devices:

> A bant'ring spirit has our men possessed,
> And wisdom is become a standing jest.
> Wit does of virtue sure destruction make;
> Who can produce a wit and not a rake?
> Wise magistrates lewd wit do therefore hate,
> The bane of virtue's treason to the state.
> While honor fails and honesty decays,

4

In vain we beat our heads for means and ways.
What well-formed government or state can last,
When wit has laid the people's virtue waste?[4]

Satire depends on the creation of a bond between author and reader *against* some third party. In their influential periodicals *The Tatler* and *The Spectator*, Addison and Steele opposed the indiscriminate deployment of wit and downgraded satire as an artistic form of expression. They sponsored 'sublime', awe-inspiring writing that, whatever its worthwhile qualities, certainly did not exhibit a sense of humour. Women did write occasional satire – Lady Mary Wortley Montagu, for example, could use it to devastating effect – but the moves that satire required a writer to make were entirely inimical to the developing ideologies of femininity and sentimentality. Women were not supposed to laugh at their fellow creatures or to have opinions strong enough to lead them into ridiculing institutions or concepts. The growing influence of benevolist psychologies based on sympathy, on the belief that the existential gap between one isolated human being and another could be overcome by exposing oneself to feel what the other feels, generated anti-satirical manifestos. As will be argued in Chapter 1, the earliest effects of this backlash against satire were felt in the theatre, where campaigns were mounted against the muscular satirical comedies of the reign of Charles and the attempts made by dramatists of the 1690s to restore them.

The early development of the novel is intimately bound up with the growing market for reading and writing imaginative literature, with the central place of women in that process, and with the possibilities for exploring sympathetic understanding of other human beings that extended prose fiction offered. The key satirists of the eighteenth century, Swift and Pope especially, regarded the effloration of what they usually termed 'romance' as an undesirable trend. In 'Grub Street', they created a powerful and enduring mythology of the conditions under which such subliterary genres were manufactured. Grub Street was an actual location situated in the north-west corner of the City of London, but in Pope's *Dunciad* it becomes a metonymy for shabby, rapidly produced prints manufactured

5

by an industry that possesses none of the qualifications of leisure and study required for writing serious literature. The deregulation of literature, the commodification of writing and the augmented possibilities for living off one's wits, was not welcomed in conservative quarters and it provided writers of a satirical bent with one of their main sources of inspiration. The major satirists of post-1688 England who are covered in Chapters 2 and 3 were all profoundly counter-cultural figures. They were square pegs in round holes. They were not impressed by the claims being made for rising prosperity, for greater comfort, for the value inherent in the widespread dissemination of print. An era of peace and commercial progress spearheaded by decades of Whig ascendancy after the fall of the Tory ministry in 1714 and the death of Queen Anne did not provide them with the opportunities they sought; and they were convinced that such a government could produce only mediocrity. Government-sponsored science, scholarship, and culture was producing a toxic compound of bad politics and bad art that it was their business to oppose. Satire was the final weapon in the armoury of a nation whose politicians, lawyers, clergymen, and creative writers had succumbed to the drug-induced sleep of the suborned.

Characteristic of the literature that in Chapter 3 is called 'Scriblerian' is its confusingly hilarious tendency to borrow the clothes of those writers and literary forms that it simultaneously wants to pillory. Swift, Pope, Gay, and Fielding all advertise the fact that their literature is parodic, made out of pasted-up strips of the writing that they want to expose as ridiculous. Their works are often presented with extended annotations conferred by a fictitious heavy-handed, pompous literary editor – Martinus Scriblerus is the most pervasive of those invented scholars – byzantine machineries of comments and remarks. Notes to the text are an independent source of comedy, and, given the typographical complexities that they make for, they implicate the book as physical object in the satirical enterprise. In the mature satire of the period the reader senses not just a will to expose and ridicule its targets but also an immersion in them. Swift's coprophilic infatuations have often been commented upon. Pope usually gets off more lightly, but there is as much interest in faecal matter in his poetry as in Swift's writing. When in Book II of *The Dunciad* he sends the dunces down into the sewers for a muck-diving competition, the poet is down and dirty with them, his imagination relishing their embrowning. The great satirists of the early eighteenth century succeeded in extracting and recycling for their own ideological purposes the energies of those writers and literary forms that they wanted to persuade us were destroying civilization. That the rude barbarian hordes were on the march and putting out the lights of civilized life is a recurring cultural nightmare, but it is given differing rhetorics of presentation at different historical junctures. The claim I would make for 'Scriblerian' satire is that this nightmare has never before or since been presented with such comedy and verve.

1

Restoration Satire

In 1683 the poet John Oldham died. Oldham had helped to put
satire on the map when he titled a major collection of poems
Satyrs upon the Jesuits – written in the 1670s when anti-Catholic
feeling was running very high, and published in 1681. This title
gives the reader the idea that satire is almost a formal exercise
in ridicule: the poet sits down, singles out a target – here,
extreme Catholicism – and sets out to destroy it systematically
in writing. In the first of the satires, in order to demonize
effectively the Catholic threat, Oldham uses as a speaker the
ghost of Henry Garnet, a Jesuit executed for his part in the
attempt to blow up James I's Parliament in 1605 known as the
Gunpowder Plot. Garnet exhorts fellow Catholics to rise up
and rebel, to suppress all human feeling and give no quarter,
in tones that are intemperate, bloodthirsty – almost deranged
with prejudice:

> Kill like a Plague or *Inquisition*; spare
> No Age, Degree, or Sex; onely to wear
> A Soul, onely to own a Life, be here
> Thought crime enough to lose 't: no time nor place
> Be Sanctuary from your outrages.
> Spare not in Churches kneeling Priests at pray'r,
> Though interceding for you, slay ev'n there.
> Spare not young Infants smiling at the brest,
> Who from relenting Fools their mercy wrest;
> Rip teeming Wombs, tear out the hated Brood
> From thence, and drown 'em in their Mothers bloud.
> .   .   .   .
> Brain the poor Cripple with his Crutch, then cry,
> You've kindly rid him of his misery.[1]

And other good-natured advice of a similar kidney! On this showing, one might infer that Oldham did not regard satire primarily as a form of art. For him, it was a rhetoric of vituperation. The Prologue he wrote for the *Satyrs* suggests that Oldham had absorbed earlier ideas to the effect that satire is propelled by the emotions of the writer – indignation, anger, and honesty supplies the ruggedness necessary for successful satire. Satire is telling it like it is: 'art' would be on a collision course with this impulse:

> 'Tis pointed Satyr and the sharps of wit
> For such a prize are th'only weapons fit:
> Nor needs there art or genious here to use,
> Where indignation can create a muse.[2]

In 1684, John Dryden contributed an elegy 'To the Memory of Mr Oldham' as a testimonial for a posthumous edition of Oldham's works. Here is the full text, omitting only the final four lines:

> Farewel, too little and too lately known,
> Whom I began to think and call my own;
> For sure our Souls were near ally'd; and thine
> Cast in the same Poetick mould with mine.
> One common Note on either Lyre did strike,
> And Knaves and Fools we both abhorr'd alike:
> To the same Goal did both our Studies drive,
> The last set out the soonest did arrive.
> Thus *Nisus* fell upon the slippery place,
> While his young Friend perform'd and won the Race.
> O early ripe! to thy abundant store
> What could advancing Age have added more?
> It might (what Nature never gives the young)
> Have taught the numbers of thy native Tongue.
> But Satyr needs not those, and Wit will shine
> Through the harsh cadence of a rugged line:
> A noble Error, and but seldom made,
> When Poets are by too much force betray'd.
> Thy generous fruits, though gather'd ere their prime
> Still shew'd a quickness; and maturing time
> But mellows what we write to the dull sweets of Rime.

(D. ii. 175, ll. 1–21)

This is an astonishing poem. As befits a funeral elegist, the poet commemorates the achievements of the deceased and situates himself in friendly rivalry. Satire traditionally excoriates 'knaves and fools': neither the deceased nor the elegist suffered them gladly, the poet infers. Dryden pays a graceful compliment to the younger man by comparing Oldham to Euryalus and himself to Nisus in the footrace described in Book V of Virgil's *Aeneid*. Though younger, the compliment goes, Oldham got there first. But where, asks the reader, did he get? To satiric achievement, or to early death? From line 11, the poem takes an unexpected direction. Lines 11–12 might be, one would think in the context of a funeral elegy, a purely rhetorical question, expecting the answer 'nothing at all'. Dryden, however, goes on to answer it. If Oldham had matured somewhat, he might actually have managed to write English poetry! Looking back on Oldham's verse in the light of this comment, we observe that, though written in couplets, the verse is so frenetically driven, so marked by enjambement (run-on lines) and irregular caesurae (pauses), as to be almost unrecognizable. Instantly, Dryden pulls back from that critical vein. 'Satire needs not those' – the essential component of satire is wit. If Oldham had faults, they were faults on the right side, and maturity inevitably carries with it a softening, almost an emasculation of youthful energy. But Dryden has made his points, and his poem contains a manifesto for the satiric art of the new age. Is it possible that Dryden intended this poem to be in itself *an example* of what satire at its best could do? Late on in his career, in 1692, Dryden translated the great Roman satires of Juvenal and Persius, and the preface he wrote for this, the *Discourse concerning the Original and Progress of Satire*, provides the most memorable image of the satirist's art to be found anywhere in the theoretical writing of the period:

> How easie it is to call Rogue and Villain, and that wittily! But how hard to make a Man appear a Fool, a Blockhead, or a Knave, without using any of those opprobrious terms! . . . there is still a vast difference betwixt the slovenly Butchering of a Man, and the fineness of a stroak that separates the Head from the Body, and leaves it standing in its place. (D. iv. 70–1)

Oldham is the slovenly butcher: Dryden the expert executioner. And as much as it is a graceful compliment to Oldham's memory, Dryden's elegy is an expert piece of execution.

10

By the time he wrote this poem, Dryden had spent several years writing theatrical prologues, the point of which was to create an atmosphere in the auditorium in which new plays would be enjoyed. He had become expert in manipulating theatres full of Restoration gallants and their ladies – melding them into audiences, making them self-conscious, enabling them to laugh at themselves and putting them in a mood to laugh at the comic fare on offer. Given Dryden's ambitions for satire – to make it into an art form and to infuse it with the mannerly, silken wit exemplified by the best Court conversation of his era – his theatrical writing was a perfect training. It is apparent in his best-known satirical poem, *Absalom and Achitophel* (1681). This poem was a direct intervention in affairs of state – what we might want to call propaganda, because its purpose is to persuade readers that King Charles II was a moderate, opposed at Court and in the city of London only by hotheads and rebels. Those who suspected that the House of Stuart leaned towards Catholicism and were trying to get the King's brother James excluded from the succession to the throne were, the poem contends, opponents of reason itself, pitting themselves against the natural and divinely sanctioned course of history. Using the story of Absalom's rebellion, in conspiracy with the evil counsellor Achitophel, against King David as told in 2 Samuel is the key to turning propaganda into art, gaining for Charles's reign biblical sanction and exploiting the reader's knowledge of David's intense but tragic love for his son to create a prevailing cadence of resigned world-weariness. From the outset, David is presented as an overindulgent father whom events force, more in sorrow than in anger, to discipline an unruly son. The long poem is studded with vivid character portraits. In the *Discourse* referred to above, Dryden had opined that the character portrait of Zimri (the Duke of Buckingham) he created in *Absalom* was 'worth the whole poem: 'tis not bloody, but 'tis ridiculous enough. And he for whom it was intended was too witty to resent it as an injury'. Here is Dryden's ideal: 'fine raillery', so well judged as to be almost a backhanded compliment to its victim. Here is the portrait:

Some of their Chiefs were Princes of the Land:
In the first Rank of these did *Zimri* stand:
A man so various, that he seem'd to be
Not one, but all Mankinds Epitome.
Stiff in Opinions, always in the wrong;
Was every thing by starts, and nothing long:
But, in the course of one revolving Moon,
Was Chymist, Fidler, States-Man and Buffoon:
Then all for Women, Painting, Rhiming, Drinking,
Besides ten thousand freaks that dy'd in thinking;
Blest Madman, who could every hour employ,
With something New to wish, or to enjoy!
Rayling and praising were his usual Theams;
And both (to shew his Judgment) in Extreams:
So over Violent, or over Civil,
That every man, with him, was God or Devil.
In squandering Wealth was his peculiar Art:
Nothing went unrewarded, but Desert.
Begger'd by Fools, whom still he found too late:
He had his Jest, and they had his Estate.

(D. ii. 21–2, ll. 543–62)

Buckingham is flattered by this at the same time as he is ridiculed. He is a dissolute dilettante, an inconsistent spend-thrift – but also energetic, versatile, endowed with a zest for living and ultimately unmalicious, 'blest madman' almost suggesting a holy fool. Dryden's formal control over the couplet, his skilful exploitation of the pause and the balanced antithesis, contrasts with the lack of self-control that is his subject. Zimri's failure to find the middle way ('every man for him was God or Devil') is a demonstration of the poem's overall critique of extremism. The poet's superior, ironic detachment renders Zimri wastefully frantic. There is exquisite wit in the zeugma through which the word for joke and that for Buckingham's worldly wealth are coupled: 'He had his jest, and they had his estate'; and the poet had the last laugh. It works almost as an 'aside' in a comic play, the poet speaking from behind his hand as his victim dances unconcerned to his ruin.

The character portrait was developed in the period by Andrew Marvell in a series of poems written in the 1660s called *The Last Instructions to a Painter*, the idea being that the text functions as a set of directions to a painter, who uses them to create a rogues' gallery of identifiable sketches. Marvell's subject in his three 'painter' poems was the satirical representation of England's conduct of the Second Dutch War, accusing the King of ruling through a petticoat government, following the lead given by his penis rather than by his intelligence. King Charles led a Court that obsessively represented its beautiful people on canvas. The King's most influential mistresses, Barbara Villiers, Countess of Castlemaine and Duchess of Cleveland, and Louise de Kéroualle, Duchess of Portsmouth, were painted again and again by Sir Peter Lely and other important painters, so that, when Marvell includes a satirical pen picture of Villiers's sexual antics with a groom in 'Last Instructions to a Painter' (1667), the metaphor of the verbal character sketch as a 'warts and all' Court painting, putting in all the blemishes the painter leaves out, was well understood by contemporary readers.

> Paint Castlemaine in colors that will hold
> (Her, not her picture, for she now grows old):
> She through her lackey's drawers, as he ran,
> Discerned love's cause and a new flame began.
> Her wonted joys thenceforth and court she shuns,
> And still within her mind the footman runs:
> His brazen calves, his brawny thighs (the face
> She slights), his feet shaped for a smoother race.
> Poring within her glass she readjusts
> Her looks and oft-tried beauty now distrusts;
> Fears lest he scorn a woman once assayed,
> And now first wished she e'er had been a maid.
> Great Love, how dost thou triumph and how reign,
> That to a groom could'st humble her disdain!
> Stripped to her skin, see how she stooping stands,
> Nor scorns to rub him down with those fair hands,
> And washing (lest the scent her crime disclose)
> His sweaty hooves, tickles him 'twixt the toes.[3]

As the Zimri portrait shows, much satire of the period has its basis in personal rivalry, deriving from political hostility or from professional jealousies that resulted from too many authors chasing too few patrons and jobs. Dryden's most celebrated satirical poem has this origin. *MacFlecknoe* (1682 though composed earlier) was the result of a literary quarrel with fellow dramatist Thomas Shadwell (?1642–92). Both were professional writers engaged in a struggle to exploit the literary marketplaces and make a living by marketing their wits, and they had been quarrelling for nearly ten years about the best way to do that. At this time, professional writing was barely respectable. Only in the professional theatre was the money motive acceptable for original composition, and, even there, writers like Dryden and Shadwell had to hitch their wagons to the reputations of the pre-Restoration greats – in particular, Shakespeare and Ben Jonson. Shadwell and Dryden were attached to different political influence groups, but their main bone of contention was about which of them was the natural successor to Ben Jonson as a playwright. That depended on how you analysed Jonson's talent. To Dryden, Jonson was the great classicist, the intellectual of the stage. He was not an especially *witty* writer, not really capable of smart dialogue. Dryden wanted to write plays in which the verbal elements, the play of linguistic intelligence, the thrust/counter-thrust of repartee, had the most prominence. Shadwell preferred visual gags, slapstick, plays that made their points through situation comedy. Whereas Shadwell's comic characters were fools, in Dryden even the comic butts tend to be intelligent. So after a decade of name calling, and argument about who stole what from whom, and about more elevated literary issues, Dryden decided to write a poem that would settle Shadwell's hash.

Now the point is that an independent literary evaluation of Shadwell's and Dryden's plays would certainly not give the verdict unequivocally to the latter. Shadwell was an excellent professional, who wrote very amusing and often successful plays. Yet generations of readers have been convinced by Dryden's *MacFlecknoe* that he was an obese, plodding, empty-noodled dunce. Dryden creates not just a portrait of Shadwell but the myth of the literary wannabe. How is the poem elevated above the status of mere name calling? *MacFlecknoe* is elevated by the structure of narrative that Dryden creates. It plays against vital cultural ceremonies like the coronation of kings (which was again looming as a major problem). The state of contemporary writing is a consistent concern, conjured up by means of systematic reference to the works of Flecknoe and Shadwell. Dryden knows their work very well and his familiarity with it enables him to build incidents from it into his own jokes. In this way, Shadwell is constructed as more than just some sad hack that Dryden hates: he becomes symbolic of the degeneration of contemporary culture. 'Shadwell' becomes a name for bad art produced by low commercial motives. The plot or fiction is as follows. There is to be a coronation. The present King of the Realm of Dulness is Richard Flecknoe (c. 1605–77), a clergyman and minor writer. But he has decided to abdicate and is looking for an appropriate heir. After a twelve-line introduction from an omniscient narrator, lines 13–63 are in soliloquy, showing how Flecknoe lights upon Shadwell as his natural successor. Flecknoe represents himself as a John the Baptist figure, a major prophet come to show the way to the one true Christ, Shadwell himself. At line 64, we cut to the actual scene and coronation day. The Barbican, then a run-down area boasting brothels and acting schools, is chosen as an appropriate setting, and lines 64–93 are devoted to describing it. This allows Dryden to compare Shadwell's literary activity to prostitution, an association of ideas that is satirically fertile. The coronation ceremony commences at line 94 and the centrepiece is the speech delivered by the abdicating King, commencing at line 139. Flecknoe's oration sets out the values of his topsy-turvy kingdom – those that Shadwell is expected to embody. Those are essentially narcissistic and self-regarding: above all, Shadwell is not to keep company with serious writers like Ben Jonson. Lines 175–210 puncture Shadwell's claims to be the 'son of Ben'. Even his huge belly, Flecknoe is made to say, is not a true resemblance to Jonson (who was 21 stone); because, whereas Jonson's corpulent frame was full of wit, Shadwell's is a 'tympany', an empty kettledrum amidst which his tiny wit sounds hollow. The poem's finale gives an idea of the multilayered jokes, the complex set of allusions that combine to make the intellectual comedy that we know as 'wit':

> He said, but his last words were scarcely heard,
> For *Bruce* and *Longvil* had a *Trap* prepar'd,
> And down they sent the yet declaiming Bard.

15

> Sinking he left his Drugget robe behind,
> Born upwards by a subterranean wind.
> The Mantle fell to the young Prophet's part,
> With double portion of his Father's Art.
>
> (D. ii. 60, ll. 211–17)

Although it is Shadwell's coronation, he has so far done none of the talking. As befits a dunce, he sits with an empty smile, while his 'father' does the talking. But father Flecknoe is finally ambushed by the stage device of opening a trapdoor and having him disappear; precisely the slapstick device that Shadwell staged in his 1676 comedy *The Virtuoso*, in which an empty and self-regarding would-be orator called Sir Formal Trifle is taken off by two smart young gallants called Bruce and Longville. So Dryden burlesques the slapstick comedy favoured by Shadwell. To extend the joke, however, Flecknoe's prophetic mantle, his 'drugget' robe, is carried upwards and rests on Shadwell, just as the Old Testament prophet Elijah is taken up to heaven on a whirlwind and his mantle passes to Elisha (2 Kgs. 2: 9–13). Flecknoe, however, goes down to where 'hell' always is in the conventional stage.

MacFlecknoe introduces us to one of the most important formal structures in this period's satire, the so-called mock-heroic. We will have more to say about this when considering the work of Alexander Pope, but Dryden's poem is a very significant and innovative example. Mock-heroic is a form that uses grandiose, inflated language to present a subject (here, the coronation of a hack writer) that is seen not to be worthy of such elevation. Comedy results from the clash between form and content. Registers of the English language are used to try to capture some of the elevation of ancient epic – of a time when heroes and great men did great deeds – applying that then to the little people and trivial actions of the present time. The poem opens thus:

> All humane things are subject to decay,
> And, when Fate summons, Monarchs must obey:
> This *Fleckno* found, who, like *Augustus*, young
> Was called to Empire, and had govern'd long:
> In Prose and Verse was own'd, without dispute
> Through all the Realms of *Non-sense*, absolute.

16

This aged Prince now flourishing in Peace,
And blest with issue of a large increase,
Worn out with business, did at length debate
To settle the succession of the State:
And pond'ring which of all his Sons was fit
To Reign, and wage immortal War with Wit;
Cry'd,'tis resolv'd; for Nature pleads that He
Should onely rule, who most resembles me:
Sh—— alone my perfect image bears,
Mature in dulness from his tender years.
Sh—— alone, of all my Sons, is he
Who stands confirm'd in full stupidity.
The rest to some faint meaning make pretence,
But Sh—— never deviates into sense.

(D. ii. 54, ll.1–20)

We begin with a sententious philosophical generalization, which is brought down to earth with the introduction of the name 'Flecknoe'. Flecknoe is then likened to Augustus. Now, we know that Augustus was an important Roman Emperor, but who in God's name was Flecknoe? Even if the contemporary reader might have known who Flecknoe was, the comparison was still ridiculous. Dryden then starts to set up his alternative, Alice-in-Wonderland kingdom, which will continue throughout the poem. This is the Empire of Nonsense, the kingdom of bad prose and verse in which Flecknoe is an absolute ruler – the phrase suggesting to English ears Louis XIV of France, despotic unenlightened dictator. Sexual innuendo will shadow the lines 'blest with issue of a large increase' and 'worn out with business'. 'Business' might be set off by pauses in the reading, to emphasize the innuendo. To contemporary readers, the legendary promiscuity of King Charles II might be evoked. Shadwell is then presented as a kind of anti-creation, made in the perfect image of his father, monumentally boring even as a young child. The final couplet uses the latinate word 'deviate' to suggest that, even by accident, Shadwell never wanders or blunders into a meaning. He is the ultimate symbol of intellectual otherness, the icon of the non-significant.

Dryden may have got the better of Shadwell, but not of John Wilmot, Earl of Rochester. With the young aristocrat, Dryden

17

had a love–hate relationship, liking to imagine himself as belonging to Rochester's circle of libertine wits but neither by birth nor by temperament suited to being so. One motive for the composition of *MacFlecknoe* was the fact that, in late 1675, Rochester had openly attacked the inadequacies both of Dryden's personality and his writing, using a new satiric form to do it. One of the most innovative of Restoration satirists, Rochester was an early English practitioner of the *imitation*, a form that would be adapted by Alexander Pope in the next century primarily for satiric purposes. Imitation began in the mid-seventeenth-century as a by-product of translation theory. Some translators of classical poetry argued that the translator should carefully modernize every line of an original for the benefit of readers who could not or would not read it in the classical language. Others, notably Cowley, argued for a less restricted way of translating that went beyond mere modernizing into the deliberate alteration of meaning to produce a different poem – an 'imitation'. Rochester's *An Allusion to Horace, the Tenth Satyr of the First Book* takes as its original Horace's *Satire 1.10*, in which he discusses the writing of satire. This, Rochester wittily adapts to his feud with John Dryden, making Horace's writers into the scribblers on the contemporary scene. This enables Rochester to provide the reader with a map of modern authorship and a set of literary values to read it by. Here are the openings, using the Everyman translation of the Horace:

> Yes I *did* say Lucilius' verses ran lamely along.
> Where can Lucilius find so fond an admirer
> As not to admit that? And yet, on the very same page,
> The same writer is praised for the way that he gave
> The city a good rubbing-down with the salt of his wit.

> Well Sir 'tis granted, I said Dryden's Rhymes
> Were stollen, unequal, nay dull many times
> What foolish Patron is there found of his
> So blindly partial to deny me this?
> But that his Plays embroyder'd up and down
> With witt and learning, justly pleasd the Town,
> In the same Paper I as freely own.

(R. 71, ll. 1–7)

Whereas Horace sticks to the literary qualities of Lucilius' satire, Rochester at once accuses Dryden of plagiarism – 'stollen' – and needles him with his need for patronage. Dryden's plays are 'embroyder'd' with wit – they are a kind of patchwork quilt. And, if they 'justly pleasd the town', so much the worse, it is implied, for the town's judgement. Rochester's imitation is much more pointed and satirical than Horace's good-natured weighing of Lucilius' talents in the balance.

Rochester took full advantage of the secular, even atheistical climate that, with his interest in Hobbesian materialism, he helped to create to satirize the King directly and to provide vivid vignettes of the ridiculous postures adopted by people acting out their social roles. Developing the formal verse satire imitated from classical models by earlier satirists like John Donne, *Tunbridge Wells* depicts the mores of the emerging spa town and shows Rochester's dramatist's ear for comic dialogue and situation. A rustic couple are wooing one another in forced compliments and ponderous small talk:

> Here waiting for Gallant, young damsell stood,
> Leaning on Cane, and Muffled up in hood.
> The would-be witt, whose buisness was to woo,
> With hat remov'd and solemn scrape of Shoe,
> Advanceth bowing, then genteelly Shruggs,
> And ruffl'd fortop into order Tuggs
> And thus accosts her: Madam, methinkes the weather
> Is grown much more serene, since you came hither.
> You Influence th'heavens, but should the sun
> Withdraw himselfe to see his rays outdone
> By your bright eyes; They would supply the Morn
> And make a day, before the day be born.
> With mouth screw'd up, conceited winking eyes,
> And breasts thrust forward; Lord! sir, she replyes,
> It is your goodness and not my deserts
> Which makes you show this learning, witt, and parts.

(R. 51–2, ll. 98–113)

In the end, after decking her out with trinkets from a peddler's stall, he gives her 'a Scotch fiddle' – a venereal disease. That is what all the conceits about her outshining the day finally arrrive at. In other more serious satirical modes, Rochester deals, not with the follies of individuals or character types, but with the pretensions to rationality of the entire human species. In *A Satyre against Reason and Mankind*, the poet invents a persona who excoriates the pretentious and the vain – those philosophers, clerics, and courtier-lawyers who terrify the less able with their intellectual bugbears about hell, damnation, and the next life. Human rationality is what frightens us and prevents us from enjoying the pleasures of this life. The 'sixth Sense', Reason, operates in opposition to the other five, and Rochester depicts it as on a journey that, through a suppressed allusion to Satan's journey in *Paradise Lost*, is represented as a diabolical departure from the one true path:

> Pathless and dangerous wandring wayes it takes,
> Through Errours fenny boggs and thorny brakes:
> Whilst the misguided follower climbs with pain
> Mountains of whimseys heapt in his own brain;
> Stumbling from thought to thought, falls headlong down
> Into doubts boundless Sea.
>
> (R. 57, ll. 14–19)

The poem's view of rationality as a satanic illusion, leading its possessor schizophrenically on to darkness and disillusioned death, and the satirist's position as almost that of a cruel, mocking deity looking down with Olympian detachment upon mankind, was read in his own time as a sneering brand of atheistical libertinism. But in this poem, Rochester makes a very serious effort to write philosophical satire, evaluating the competing claims of neo-Epicureanism against more orthodox Christian moral positions.

Everything said so far has implied a connection between the nature of post-Restoration satire and of post-Restoration society, and it is time to be more explicit about this connection. A society on the change, post-1660 England was defined in large part by the cultural memory of a decade of civil war, religious intolerance, and the subsequent experiments in republican social organization. 'Restoration', however much it was represented as a return to the familiar antebellum world of hierarchy and privilege, was not unequivocally so. Charles II was more conscious than any previous monarch of the importance of public opinion and of the vital need to make concessions to it. Presiding over a sceptical, scientific kingdom increasingly devoting itself to trade and commerce, he had often to work through negotiation and compromise. He was an 'easy' monarch, whose many mistresses could not but compromise the mystery surrounding the king's body; whose venereal behaviour attracted comment in the public theatre and in privately circulated manuscript verse. Satire could develop as the kind of art form that Dryden wished it to be, in large part because the King was prepared to tolerate it as an acceptable pressure valve. Satirical freedom of speech was part of a developing culture of commentary, disseminated in coffee houses and clubs, in theatres and in public prints. Charles understood that absolutism could not be the way forward, especially for a monarch as appetitive and carnal as himself: he could not easily take the moral high ground. Taking its cue to some extent from the monarch, Restoration sexuality was more open, by far, than it had been in the Interregnum period, and indeed than it would be again, arguably until our own time. 'Sex', says Kevin Sharpe, 'was the solvent of the boundaries of class and of the moral proprieties that had once . . . distinguished the aristocrats . . . from lesser mortals who were slaves to their passions'.[4] The squib that John Wilmot, Earl of Rochester, inadvertently handed to the King early in 1674, 'A Satyr on Charles II', can be used to illustrate a number of the points made above:

> In the Isle of Brittain, long since famous growne
> For breeding the best C——ts in Christendome,
> Not long since Reign'd (oh may he long survive)
> The easiest King and best bred Man alive.
> Him no Ambition mov'd to get Renowne
> Like a French foole still wand'ring up and downe,
> Starving his People, hazarding his Crowne.
> Peace was his Aime, his gentleness was such
> And Love, he lov'd, For he lov'd Fucking much,
> Nor was his high desire above his Strength:
> His Scepter and his Prick were of a length,
> And she may sway the one who plays with t'other,
> Which makes him litle wiser than his Brother.
> For Princes Pricks like to Buffoones at Court
> Doe governe Us, because they make Us Sport.
> His was the sauciest that did ever swive,

21

The prowdest peremptory Prick alive:
Tho Safety, Law, Religion, Life lay on't
Twould breake thro all to make it's way to C——t.
Restlesse he Rowles about from Whore to Whore
With Dogg and Bastard, always goeing before,
A merry Monarch, scandalous and poore.

(R 85–6, ll. 1–22)

Admittedly, Rochester had to flee the Court after delivering himself of this, but it is difficult to imagine that under any previous monarch he would have retained his head. Charles's Third Dutch War was not going well and by the Treaty of Westminster early in 1674, he withdrew from it, leaving Louis of France to pursue territorial ambition in his stead. The critique of Charles is clear: led by his genitals, he is leaving the serious business of state to fools and women, and the theatre of ambition open to Louis of France. Despite his sexual prowess, Charles is almost effeminate, his ease and gentleness dissolving his ability to lead the nation.

Rochester epitomized the sexual melting pot of the 1670s. He personified the self as theatre. In several plays of the decade, male actors are seen readying themselves for their day, constructing their social roles through their dress, making the journey from private self to public theatricalized being. In life, Rochester was a model for several playwrights: he is the glamorous and suave Dorimant in Etherege's *The Man of Mode* (1676), the viciously immoral Nemours in Dryden and Lee's *The Princess of Cleve* (1681–2), and the contemptibly hypocritical libertine Florio in Crowne's *City Politiques* (1682). The issue for us, however, is whether, in the kind of play for which Rochester's life served as a partial inspiration, satire is actually involved? Are the sex comedies of the Restoration, which reached their zenith in the 1670s, satires? To use a textbook definition, satire is the literary art of diminishing a subject by making it ridiculous, evoking towards it an attitude of amusement, indignation, contempt, or scorn. The target of satire might be a personal enemy, an institution like the Church or the government or the law, or even conceivably the human race, as we have seen in some of Rochester's writing. Satire is sometimes direct, spoken in the first person, and sometimes couched in the form of a narrative. And it can 'colonize' all the major literary genres – poetry, drama, and the novel – where it can occupy varying amounts of the total material. John Milton, the period's major writer, wrote many poems in which satire occurs: *Paradise Lost* (1667), *Samson Agonistes* (1671), and *Lycidas* (1637) are the salient examples; but, because satire occurs in those only locally by topic or as the result of a briefly adopted tone of voice, we need not focus on his writing in an account of the period's satire. Restoration comic theatre is, however, a very problematic case, because it is not clear whether the plays are glorifying or holding up to scorn the behaviours that they represent. How do they map onto the social realities that they mediate? Do they, as Restoration dramatists frequently claimed, simply reflect back to the audience the social behaviour that was its own? If they edit, or distort, or schematize that behaviour, do they do this by *glorifying* it or by *ridiculing* it? Is Restoration comedy satire or celebration?

Take an example: William Wycherley's 1675 play *The Country Wife*. In this play, the protagonist Horner has it rumoured that he is sexually disabled due to some unspecified mishap in France, so that he will be trusted by other husbands as a kind of eunuch-companion to their wives. The extent to which those wives find him nauseating will be a kind of litmus test of how much they actually like illicit sex. What kind of plausibility does a plot device like this have? There is some kind of psychology operating here, or perhaps it is better termed a sociology? Women love sex outside marriage, and, if a man is known to be *hors de combat*, they will abominate him. Men are happy to give sexually disabled men free access to their wives. It seems inherently unlikely that significant numbers of people in Restoration society actually thought like this! One notices further that some of the male and female characters in the play are actually constructed along certain schematic lines of symmetry. While the jealous Pinchwife guards his wife and will not let her out of his sight, the easy and foppish Sparkish is eager to push his fiancée Alithea into the company of Harcourt to show how free from jealousy he is. Do 'real' men and women turn up in inverted copies of one another? On closer inspection, it seems that Restoration sex comedies offer,

23

not 'reality', but a carefully edited, stripped-down model of the way in which society works: and only the way it works in highly selective social groupings and departments of life. The sex comedies of the 1670s present identifiable characters operating in stock situations, offering a limited range of attitudes towards marriage: husbands and wives never get along; marriage is merely a civil contract, never anything deeper; constancy in love is a bore; sexual appetite requires the constant stimulus of the chase; cuckoldom is the worst fate that can overtake a man; every woman wishes to commit adultery, and will if she can do so without being found out. Sex comedies of the period represent life as a game, the objective of which is successfully concealed adultery. The hero is a rake, a young man who has no visible means of support and feels no imperative to earn a living, and who is as excited by playing the game as by winning it. His wit is a weapon in the sex war, an aid to seduction. He and his scheming female counterparts know the rules of the game and exploit them to take advantage of society's endemic hypocrisy and double standard. He is counterpointed to the fop – the false wit, who mistakes the rules of the game for its objective. He does not realize that wit, and fine clothes, are not ends in themselves but simply tools of the trade. His female equivalent is a lustful older woman, ludicrously conceited and deluded as to her continuing sexual charms. Sometimes, as in *The Country Wife*, there are characters who are naive or fresh or who in other respects do not fit in – country bumpkins who do not understand the game at all: they have some inkling that there is pleasure to be gained from it and try very hard to learn it. And there are heavy fathers and mothers, and cuckolds who always think they are ahead of the game and always lose. The sex comedies of the 1670s do have satirical scenes in them, where the behaviour of the characters is so louche and carnal that the dramatic point lies in exposure. By the end of Act II of *The Country Wife*, Horner has taken selected women into his confidence, and there is a memorable scene that has come to stand almost symbolically for the entirety of this theatrical repertoire, the so-called china scene (Act IV, Scene iii), in which Horner is virtually caught *in flagrante* by Sir Jaspar Fidget with his wife, but quickly takes up her spur-of-the-moment pretence that he is an expert on china, who runs a kind of porcelain shop out of his lodgings. At once, 'china' becomes a nonce metaphor for sexual gratification, or semen: and soon Mrs Squeamish is knocking on the door demanding 'china'. Jokes about 'coming in the back way' abound, as 'china' comes to symbolize the reality of base clay beneath painted exteriors – a metaphor for contemporary society. Overall, though, the ascendancy of the rake hero in the comedies of the 'high' Restoration maintains them as celebrations of youth over age, of wit over business, of leisure over employment, and of the aristocrat over the middle-status 'citizen'. They are not primarily satirical, because they do not have, even as a conventional aspiration, the reform of society as an intention. If sexual–marital relations in contemporary society are as the plays show them to be, 'better to be a winner than a loser' seems to be the moral. I have sometimes suspected in *The Country Wife* a layer of political satire. The whoremongering Horner, prepared to compromise his virility in the venereal cause, stirred at the prospect of hunting down a naive country wench, might conceal a reference to the King: unsuccessful in his foreign campaigns, his political potency compromised by devotion to pleasure and the pursuit of mistresses, some lowborn, like the actress Nell Gwyn, and several represented as shepherdesses on canvas. If so, that is too deeply buried in the play's 'political unconscious' to be an open target of satire.

If we fast forward to the last decade of the century, however, we find a very different picture. In the 1690s, the major dramatists Southerne, Congreve, and Vanbrugh fought a rearguard action against a moral reform movement the tendency of which was to remove from public exhibition all representations of behaviour deemed immoral. The playwrights fought their corner by arguing that the plays had an explicitly satirical intention. Jeremy Collier's *A Short View of the Profaneness and Immorality of the English Stage* (1698) exemplifies the new taste of the rising people of the middle station in life: this is what he has to say, for example, about the rake hero of the comedies of Congreve and Vanbrugh:

> To sum up the Evidence. A fine Gentleman is a fine Whoring, Swearing, Smutty, Atheistical Man. These Qualifications, it seems,

compleat the *Idea* of Honour. They are the Top-Improvements of Fortune, and the distinguishing Glories of Birth and Breeding! . . . the Restraints of Conscience and the Pedantry of Virtue are unbecoming a Cavalier. Future Securities and Reaching beyond Life are vulgar Provisions. If he falls a thinking at this Rate, he forfeits his Honour; For his Head was only made to run against a Post! Here you have a Man of Breeding and Figure that burlesques the *Bible*, Swears, and talks Smut to Ladies, speaks ill of his Friend behind his Back, and betraies his Interest: A Fine Gentleman . . . fine only in the Insignificancy of Life, the abuse of Religion, and the Scandals of Conversation.[5]

Goaded by the new anti-theatrical puritanism of clergymen such as Jeremy Collier, dramatists asserted that their art was a kind of aversion therapy. We might adduce a number of reasons for the change in the moral temperature in the 1690s. One of them was a considerable widening of the audience base, when a hugely enlarged Drury Lane Theatre designed by Wren was reopened in 1672 after a fire. To fill that theatre required an art appealing much more widely to the emerging solid, respectable middle-class citizens of London. In Dryden's 1672 comedy *Marriage à la Mode*, this section of the community is ridiculed by the affected Court hanger-on Melantha, and, in all the plays of the 1670s, citizens are ludicrous oafs whose taste for profit and business prevents them from satisfying their wives or stopping others from doing so. The prevalence of middle-class taste over theatrical programming was a gradual process, but it received a huge boost in 1688 with the accession of King William III. If the sex comedy of the 1670s had taken its complexion from the lascivious habits of Charles II, the homosexually inclined and yet deeply uxorious William was a very different animal. Given the deep unpopularity of William's reign, it was early perceived by the clergymen who surrounded him that his reign needed spin. William III and his consort Mary used a 'clean-up society' campaign for moral reform as one means of legitimizing a reign that did not seem legitimate to many English people. It was an attempt to capture the hearts and minds of solid middle-station burghers, a public-relations initiative pursued through Royal proclamation and the sermons and writings of the higher clergy. The effect of William's campaign in the 1690s was to politicize the personal. Towards the end of the decade, the Commons was thanking the King for his declaration of an intention to discourage profanity and immorality, 'which chiefly by the neglect and ill example of too many magistrates are like a general contagion diffused and spread throughout the kingdom'. The temper of the times is epitomized in this zealous attempt to render the ethical conduct of individuals within marriage the legitimate province of the law.

Against this general milieu, the 'marital disharmony' comedies of Congreve and Vanbrugh must be understood. Vanbrugh was tempted into writing for the theatre by a perceived need to take a stand against a constraining and unconvincing view of marital relations that threatened to make it impossible for comedy to perform its age-old mission: of making us laugh at things as they are. The postures of older sex comedy, such as held the stage for a while in the 1670s and 1680s but influenced the popular imagination for much longer, were far too brittle for a society beginning to accept that married couples really had to find a way to live fulfilled lives together. We can exemplify this by *The Provoked Wife* (1697), Vanbrugh's second play. It focuses on a married couple, Sir John and Lady Brute. The husband is a boorish, whoring, hard-drinking atheist whose only reason for getting married is that his wife would not sleep with him if he did not. She has married him for his money. Sir John's hatred for the married state has grown into a predominant humour, the motivating force of his drunken, dissolute conduct. His desire to beat women is a minor leitmotif in the play, and there are two scenes in which he is represented with his cronies attacking and robbing innocent bystanders, impersonating the clergy, and behaving with appalling insubordination towards the bench: all this he does in the name of 'liberty and property' – a Whig slogan quite meaningless coming from his lips because his tendencies are entirely anarchic, or absolutist, except when it comes to protecting his own property in his wife. From the opening scene, Lady Brute is constructing arguments to persuade herself that, in such circumstances as Brute provides, the marriage vows cannot mean anything. Her lover Constant does not encounter much resistance therefore. In Act III, Scene i, Constant argues that virtue cannot be equated with sexual continence, but is a far more charitable, extroverted, active quality. Lady Brute is persuaded and in Act IV, Scene iv, it is made absolutely clear that she would have yielded to Constant in the arbour in Spring Garden if they had not been interrupted by the spying Lady Fancyfull. Strictly speaking, Sir John is not cuckolded; but his other predominant character trait is cowardice, and Constant makes it icily clear that, should he ever choose to question his wife's constancy, he is likely to end up as a kebab. He leaves Sir John in Act V, Scene ii, to consider the injustice of thus being made a compliant cuckold, with which the audience might have some sympathy if earlier in the scene Sir John had not committed a virtual rape upon his wife and if he had not fallen asleep before he finishes his meditation. In Act V, Scene v, in another Falstaffian speech, he accepts the terms of the unstated treaty the men make. Discretion is the better part of valour. He will ask no awkward questions in the interests of staying alive – now, or (it is implied) in future.

This I think we can regard as a properly satirical play, because in holding the Brutes up to ridicule it implies that, as Vanbrugh says, 'there are an infinity of Husbands who have a very great share of [Brute's] Vices'. The nuptial state is more like Life with the Brutes than it is like the affectionate idyll that the religious majority would wish it to be. *The Provoked Wife* does have a clear reformist purpose. It is stated more than once in the play that Lady Brute should have access to a remedy at law – to divorce. What, in the current state of the marriage laws and canons, is a woman tempted as Lady Brute is tempted supposed to do? Under attack by Collier, Vanbrugh wrote a pamphlet in his plays' defence entitled *A Short Vindication of* The Relapse *and* The Provok'd Wife *from Immorality and Prophaneness* (1697), in which he raises the question of moral reform:

> What I have done is in general a Discouragement to Vice and Folly; I am sure I intended it, and I hope I have performed it . . . The real Query is, Whether the Way I have varied [from the normal remedies given by clergymen and physicians], be likely to have a good Effect, or a bad one? That's the true State of the Case; which if I am cast in, I don't question however to gain at least thus much of my Cause, That it shall be allow'd I aim'd at the Mark, whether I hit it or not.[6]

Against the differing cultural background of the 1690s, in the light of the 'clean-up theatre' campaign of Jeremy Collier and his band of moral crusaders, Vanbrugh had to consider – could not avoid considering – the moral tendency of his art. Behind the representation of social behaviour in his plays is a self-conscious analysis of the shortcomings in social structure that are in part responsible for the behaviour. This sustained analysis is what makes the play different from the sex comedies of the earlier generation, though those were certainly satirical on occasion. Vanbrugh was provoked into writing for the theatre by an interest in the nature of temptation, the power of human desires, and their ability to elude mechanisms like marriage designed to curb and control them. He would go on to be the architect behind such famous English buildings as Castle Howard and Blenheim Palace.

2

Alexander Pope

On 2 November 1741, the young actor later to become the most famous of all eighteenth-century performers, David Garrick, was appearing in the fifth performance of his *Richard III*. He was told that a celebrity was in the house – the famous poet Alexander Pope. To his friend Percival Stockdale he described his feelings:

> When I was told that POPE was in the house, I instantaneously felt a palpitation at my heart; a tumultuous, not a disagreeable emotion in my mind. I was then in the prime of youth; and in the zenith of my theatrical ambition. It gave me particular pleasure that RICHARD was my character, when pope was to see, and hear me. As I opened the part, I saw our little poetical hero, dressed in black, seated in a side-box near the stage; and viewing me with a serious, and earnest attention. His look shot, and thrilled, like lightning through my frame; and I had some hesitation in proceeding, from anxiety, and from joy.[1]

James Boswell described a further incident dating from 1742, two years before the poet's death, when he attended an auction of his friend Edward Harley's pictures. The room clearing almost like the Red Sea parting as Pope walked through it gives some idea of the extraordinary, almost sacred esteem in which the poet was held by the latter stages of his life. Pope was what we would call a 'celebrity', someone with whom everyone wanted skin contact: 'The room was much crowded. Pope came in. Immediately it was mentioned he was there, a lane was made for him to walk through. Everyone in the front rows by a kind of enthusiastic impulse shook hands with him.'[2]

How did Alexander Pope come to be a 'little poetical hero'? On first consideration, Pope seems more naturally to be a victim of satire than a perpetrator of it. Disabled and deformed by a tubercular condition contracted in early childhood that left him less than a metre and a half tall; a Roman Catholic at a time when Protestantism established its ascendancy and therefore not able to have the benefit of a university education or to own property; unmarried and childless, Pope does not seem well equipped for the business of ridiculing, dissecting, and exposing others. The fascination of Pope's career is the way in which he turned weakness into strength, marginality into centrality.

Pope's reputation as the greatest satirist of the age was founded on an extreme version of the argument that we saw Vanbrugh and the other Restoration playwrights propounding in the previous chapter. The playwrights were forced to defend their art on the grounds that (1) it was an accurate representation of 'the way we live now' and (2), in being so, it had a reformist moral tendency. It was not the corrupting, anticlerical, carnal art that Jeremy Collier and others took it to be; its social effect was salubrious. What can be wrong with art that is truthful? How can writers be criticized for telling it like it is, and especially if they do so wittily and entertainingly? To be effective, to distinguish itself from lampoon or name calling or mere insult, satire has to be accurate and ethical. Such a view of satire was the one that Pope developed, throughout the length of his career. Crucial to this was the development of an entirely distinctive poetic voice, an instantly recognizable, unmistakable personality, the keynote of which was *independence*. This is how Pope markets his marginality and disadvantage as a positive privilege. Constructing himself as an outsider, uninterested in power or patronage, a non-metropolitan figure who, retiring to his suburban fastness in Twickenham, can view the follies of Court, city, and government – a creative artist who, like Oscar Wilde, has nothing to declare but his genius – Pope can persuade us that he stands outside all the interest groups that polarize his society. If he can impress upon his readers that he is in no one's pocket, that he owes allegiance to no potentate or party, he can make his own unimpeachable life underwrite the ethical truth of his writing. Mythologizing the self goes hand in hand with making myths out of others, both his enemies and his friends. Over the years,

31

Pope's satire creates a gallery of heroes and villains, his verse peppered with proper names that point not just at living individuals – particular men and women – but names that come to stand as symbols for timeless qualities of good and evil, virtue and vice.

Before looking at the development of Pope's career over time, it might be useful to give an example of the above in action. Sir Richard Blackmore, Physician to King William, might serve as a talismanic example of the temper of the 1690s, the era in which the precocious Pope had his boyhood. In the preface to his vast epic *Prince Arthur* (1695), Blackmore informs the reader that his motive for writing an epic is concern at the state of contemporary letters: 'Our Poets seem engag'd in a general *Confederacy* to ruin the End of their own Art, to expose *Religion* and *Virtue*, and bring *Vice* and *Corruption of Manners* into esteem and reputation . . .'.[3]

Blackmore goes on to defend the 'Diligent, Thriving *Citizen*', the Alderman, and the JP from the merciless ridicule of contemporary comedy, and thinks that poets and preachers ought to be kept under a rigid system of state licensing. Blackmore thus allies himself with the philistine and small-minded moral rearmament campaign being spearheaded by the monarch and by influential sections of the clergy. For selling itself in this way to the Whig ascendancy, his writing was enshrined in Pope's satire as a prime example of venal, deadened art. As late as 1733, in a version of the Roman satirist Horace's *Satire* II.i (First Satire of the Second Book) that Pope composed as a dialogue with an unidentified friend (FR.), Pope is still using Blackmore as his prime example of the artist who has sold out to the military state. After William III, he transfers his talents to the Georges and the House of Brunswick. In answer to his friend's suggestion that he should write poetry in praise of the King, to attract rewards like a knighthood or the poet laureateship (Bays):

> FR. Or if you needs must write, write CAESAR's Praise:
> You'll gain at least a *Knighthood*, or the *Bays*.
>
> (P. 614, ll. 21–2)

Pope replies witheringly:

P. What? like Sir *Richard*, rumbling, rough and fierce,
WITH ARMS, AND GEORGE, AND BRUNSWICK crowd the verse?
Rend with tremendous Sound your ears asunder,
With Gun, Drum, Trumpet, Blunderbuss & Thunder?

(P. 614, ll. 21–6)

The catalogue of names and proper nouns associates Blackmore with a poetry of sound and fury, dissonant and meaningless in its anxiety to please its political paymasters.

Pope's early and late career is divided by a long period of around ten years (1715–25) during which he wrote very little that was original, spending his time instead translating the Homeric epics into approachable couplet verse and making Shakespeare's plays accessible in a new edition. That unbearably grinding labour established the poet not just as a rich man – the first writer to amass a personal fortune through his work – but as the foremost cultural broker of the age. Pope carried the high literary art of ancient Greece and Elizabethan England to a public not skilled in reading such works for themselves or in the original language, achieving for himself an impregnable position as a cultural leader. Pope's own view of his career as given in his verse autobiography, the *Epistle to Dr Arbuthnot*, was that it did divide into two phases, pre- and post-satirical:

That not in Fancy's Maze he wander'd long,
But stoop'd to Truth, and moraliz'd his song;

(P. 608, ll. 340–1)

the word 'stoop'd' ironically suggesting that, in a venal age, moral verse will be regarded as less worthwhile than purely imaginative and escapist poetry. In fact, Pope had from the outset a satirical temperament and was always drawn to such ways of expressing himself. What he developed during and after his translation phase was a social and cultural analysis that staked claims for the importance and seriousness of his poetic vision, and the power to have this analysis heard. It was in essence a 'manichaean' vision – one suggesting that the world is divided into two principles of good and evil: as he puts it in the *Epilogue to the Satires*, 'Ask you what Provocation I have had? | The strong Antipathy of Good to Bad' (ll. 197–8). In what remains

33

of this chapter, we will chart Pope's developing analysis, illustrating its execution in verse and in the process showing how the poetic embodiment of this potent ideology captured the high ground from his enemies.

Pope was, as I have said, temperamentally attracted to satirical forms of expression. When paraphrasing Chaucer as an early exercise, for example, it is to the story of January and May and to the Wife of Bath's Prologue that the poet is drawn. Now, the Wife of Bath's history of her sex life is not, perhaps, a subject that one might expect the wholly inexperienced 16 year old to want to put in his own words. The Wife's somewhat middle-aged account of the ebbs and flows of marital passion and of her libido management, reset by Pope into couplets, seems to be even more pointed than is the original. His version brings out amusingly the Wife's *de haut en bas* treatment of her husband – 'Approach my Spouse . . .' – and her turning the biblical tables against him by deploying the Job exemplum. Pope's version reads more like a theatrical vignette than Chaucer's, more like a performance script where the reader can envisage the blocking-out of every gesture and movement:

> '*Billy*, my dear! how sheepishly you look!
> Approach my Spouse, and let me kiss thy Cheek;
> Thou should'st be always thus, resign'd and meek!
> Of *Job*'s great Patience since so oft you preach,
> Well shou'd you practise, who so well can teach.
> 'Tis difficult to do, I must allow,
> But I, my dearest, will instruct you how.
> Great is the Blessing of a prudent Wife,
> Who puts a Period to Domestick Strife!
> One of us two must rule, and one obey,
> And since in Man right Reason bears the Sway,
> Let that frail Thing, weak Woman, have her way.
> Fye, 'tis unmanly thus to sigh and groan;
> What? would you have me to your self alone?
> Why take me Love! take all and ev'ry part!
> Here's your Revenge! you love it at your Heart.
> Would I vouchsafe to sell what Nature gave,
> You little think what Custom I cou'd have!
> But see! I'm all your own – nay hold – for Shame!
> What means my Dear – indeed – you are to blame.'

> (P. 103–4, ll. 183–204)

The dialectic between male and female, ruling and obeying, reason and passion, sole possession and public sale, is economically and tersely played out in this version. Pope's exploitation of the pause (caesura) to suggest husband Billy's attempts to gain his conjugals in exchange for accepting the Wife's authority over him renders the Wife even more manipulative than she is in Chaucer. Pope's early exercises one wants to mark at alpha plus – a very promising debut.

Much of Pope's early poetry is characterized by a satiric impulse that gets hold even of poems that do not set out to be satirical in any way. *An Essay on Criticism*, published in 1711 when Pope was 23, was the first poem to make his name, though his *Pastorals*, published in Tonson's *Miscellanies* in 1709, were noted. The main point of *An Essay* is to give advice on how to write poetry and how to read it, astonishingly audacious coming from a young man who has not really earned his spurs in either as yet. But the poem is ambushed (and, to my mind, rescued from what can be numbing sententiousness) by its desire to represent the current literary scene as in danger of being overrun by deranged scribblers. This is the beginning of a world view that will become very central to Pope's satiric voice. It has its origins in the intellectual ferment of the late seventeenth and early eighteenth centuries, and a full discussion of it will be reserved for the next chapter. Suffice it to say here that the expansion of the market for writing and reading in this period produced in writers of a conservative stamp considerable anxiety about quality control. If literary composition is a vocation rather than a trade, if it is the product of long hours of education and study, how can it be the province of every fool who takes it into his head to pick up a pen? A poem to some extent written as a 'how to do it' manual for aspiring writers is haunted by the anxiety that actually there are far too many of them trying to do it, and they would be better off as butchers, bakers, and candlestick-makers. At one point in the *Essay*, Pope takes the fatal step of ridiculing the influential writer and critic John Dennis under the nickname Appius (after the title of one of his plays). He does not need to do this – the poem does not demand it – but he crosses the rubicon into personal satire:

> 'Twere well, might Criticks still this Freedom take;
> But *Appius* reddens at each Word you speak,
> And *stares, Tremendous!* with a *threatning Eye,*
> Like some *fierce Tyrant* in *Old Tapestry!*

> (P. 162, ll. 584–7)

'Tremendous' was one of Dennis's favourite critical terms. Pope here catches Dennis's unbalanced enthusiasm of expression, the brilliantly wounding simile comparing him to something you might see in a Gobelin hanging on the wall of a great house, staring because it is difficult to do natural expressions in tapestry. This stroke of personal satire in some ways set the agenda for the rest of Pope's career. It commenced a war of Trojan proportions with Dennis, writers in his circle, and very many others who might have been Whiggish in their politics or envious of Pope's success or otherwise eager to halt his professional advancement. It was to lead to Pope's most significant achievement in verse, when he finally decided to settle the score with them, the 1728/9 *Dunciad*. In the meantime, Pope's poems continued to be surprised by satire. Building again on Chaucer, Pope's *The Temple of Fame* (1715) starts off as a visionary 'allegory', but, as Fame gives way to slander or false fame, and as those heroes deserving of fame give place to groups who clearly do not deserve it and whose approach to the Goddess of Fame is unwarranted, the poem takes on a satiric cast. Its vision gradually darkens, as fame or good reputation comes to seem impossible to achieve in a world where lies and rumour are inseparable from true fame. Some suspect that running through much of Pope's pre-1715 poetry is a hidden vein of political satire. In *The Temple of Fame*, this is quite likely, given the trouble Pope takes to defend 'allegory' (by which he means a 'fable' or narrative having a layer of moral significance) in the long prefatory note. That elaboration almost seems to suggest that readers should look for such possibilities. A passage such as this:

> Last, those who boast of mighty Mischiefs done,
> Enslave their Country, or usurp a Throne;
> Or who their Glory's dire Foundation laid,
> On Sovereigns ruin'd, or on Friends betray'd,

> Calm, thinking Villains, whom no Faith cou'd fix,
> Of crooked Counsels and dark Politicks . . .
>
> (P. 185, ll. 406–11)

although it names no names, certainly seems to glance at the triumph of Williamite Whiggery. Poems like this, however, were knocked into a cocked hat by the appearance, first in 1712 in a two-canto version, and then in 1714 in the grand five-canto version, of *The Rape of the Lock*.

The gestation of this celebrated poem is well known. Pope was approached by one of his Catholic neighbours, John Caryll, to write something that might help to smooth the ruffled feathers of the Fermor family. The daughter, Arabella (Bell), had been insulted by a young nobleman, Lord Petre, who had cut off a lock of her hair and was boasting about it as if it were a great triumph and as if Bell Fermor was the kind of girl who welcomed such intimacy. Pope's solution was to make much ado about nothing. Using the structure of classical and modern epic (Homer, Virgil, Milton) to shape the very domestic incidents of this quarrel, Pope puts into a certain perspective the high-society spat that is his subject. Epic memorializes the heroic events and personalities that built ancient empires. It inscribes the dominant myths, legends, and religious cults of warlike peoples. The grandeur of epic, its invocation to the Muse, its hero who embodies the cardinal virtues of the society, the military incidents, active intervention of the deities into the lives of mortals, omens, portents, and prophecies, the obligatory trip to the underworld: all of this is shadily present in *The Rape of the Lock* as a world that is missing – just out of reach. Pope represents Arabella Fermor in the poem under the name of Belinda. We seem to be watching Belinda's world through the wrong end of a telescope. Everything seems to be miniaturized. Social forms taken very seriously by the participants appear to the reader like life in an animated doll's house. Part of this is the effect of the supernatural beings in the poem, what in Pope's day would be called its epic 'machinery'. For those creatures, Pope went to a French work of Rosicrucian lore called *Le Comte de Gabalis*, where he found sylphs, gnomes, nymphs, and salamanders. In his treatment of them, though, this order of being has much in common with native English fairies and sprites – the indigenous folklore employed by Shakespeare, for example, in *Midsummer Night's Dream* for Titania and Oberon. Although it is often said that Pope's brand of 'mock-epic' is not a mockery *of* epic, that the critique all goes in one direction – so that the epic world is used to show the triviality and small-mindedness of English society that could regard this storm in a teacup as important – I would want to challenge that view. *The Rape of the Lock* could be written at all only because epic itself was being perceived as faintly ridiculous. Sir Richard Blackmore, whose epics have been mentioned earlier in the chapter, was in part responsible for this, because they were such bourgeois and in some ways clodhopping attempts to write epic for his own times. They weakened the hold of epic on the popular imagination, in a way that the great translations of Dryden and Pope himself did not do. In a literary agenda that was becoming increasingly domestic, at a time when the English novel was getting off the ground essentially to carry that agenda forward, the heroic poses of epic could seem stiff and stilted. The Cave of Spleen episode in Pope's *Rape* is a burlesque of the journey to the underworld motif from epic. After the cutting-off of her hair in Canto III, the care of Belinda is transferred from Ariel the sylph to Umbriel the gnome. This flags up a sense that Belinda is now in a hysterical condition. Umbriel's journey to the Cave of Spleen in Canto IV is a journey into a monstrous womb that represents the dark side of Belinda's sexualized imagination. We move from the real into the surreal, almost a world of premenstrual tension. Spleen herself is presented as a creature of pain and headache, while the strange Daliesque inhabitants of the Cave might have been petrified into stiff, absurd postures by sexual frustration:

> Unnumber'd Throngs on ev'ry side are seen
> Of Bodies chang'd to various Forms by *Spleen*.
> Here living *Teapots* stand, one Arm held out,
> One bent; the Handle this, and that the Spout:
> A Pipkin there like *Homer's Tripod* walks;
> Here sighs a Jar, and there a Goose-pye talks;
> Men prove with Child, as pow'rful Fancy works,
> And Maids turn'd Bottels, call aloud for Corks.

> (P. 233– 4, iv. 47–54)

This is the epic underworld Freudianized. It is a projection of Belinda's fantasy world, into which she is pitched by a sense that, in losing her crucial ringlet, she has been symbolically deflowered.

Celebratory as the poem is of the dazzling beauty of surfaces, Pope retains the sense that something *hinges* on all of this; that it *matters*. The poem is not merely the free play of the imagination; it also retains a strong moral awareness. What that 'something' is is not altogether congenial to generations of feminist-influenced readers, I fear. There is satire at the expense of a society that, however attractive and glitzy its surface, has lost touch with real values. Zeugma, the trope that links together nouns of different moral weight by the same verb ('When Husbands, or when Lapdogs, breathe their last'; 'Or stain her Honour, or her new Brocade'; 'Dost sometimes Counsel take, and sometimes Tea'), is the figure that often carries this moral freight. This kind of satire 'shines on all alike', to use Pope's own phrase. It is as critical of men as it is of women. A Court that wastes its time in cards, coffee drinking, and amorous spats is being mocked, though not with a heavy hand. Pope still gives full weight to the Watteauesque beauty of the social whirl, as embodied in the transcendent attractiveness of the heroine Belinda.

But there is, I think, a less attractive poem trying to get out. After the set-piece description in Canto I of Belinda 'arming for battle', beautifying herself and sacrificing to the cosmetic powers – the moral critique ever present in the narcissistic implications of worshipping her own image in the mirror and performing the 'sacred Rites of Pride' – Canto II sends her into society carrying a parody crucifix. It is really an ornament, not a religious symbol. Belinda's 'unfixed' eyes and her unsettling ability to 'shine on all alike' underline a motif of lack of discrimination, a refusal to pair-bond, that the poem seems to want to tame. The central terms of the 'rape' in III.125 ff. are unpleasantly reminiscent of some eighteenth-century por-nography. If the passage is read emphasizing all of those words that have, or could possibly have, a sexualized double entendre, there seems to be almost the atmosphere of a brothel created. Belinda is drugged up on coffee and not, perhaps, fully in control of her faculties. Handing over the scissors to the Baron, Clarissa acts almost as a kind of brothel-madam. Critics argue about the significance of Clarissa's being the Baron's helper here. In the very final version of the poem (1717), which adds Clarissa's moral passage in Canto V, she seems almost to have a normative function, almost to be the poet's representative in the poem. Some years earlier, in a poem sent to one of Pope's women who got away, the beautiful Teresa Blount (*Epistle to Miss Blount, with the Works of Voiture* (c.1710)), Pope had in a somewhat threatening manner already preached Clarissa's lesson:

> But, Madam, if the Fates withstand, and you
> Are destin'd *Hymen*'s willing Victim too,
> Trust not too much your now resistless Charms,
> Those, Age or Sickness, soon or late, disarms;
> *Good Humour* only teaches Charms to last,
> Still makes new Conquests, and maintains the past:
> Love, rais'd on Beauty, will like That decay,
> Our Hearts may bear its slender Chain a Day.
>
> (P. 170, ll. 57–64)

This seems to be what Pope wants to say to beautiful women. 'You may be in the ascendant now, but your beauty won't last. The only way to fend off the fate that usually befalls former beauties is to cultivate those gifts that can attract and retain men's affections over the longer term.' Clarissa's handing over of the scissors to cut the lock is therefore an act of taming quite consistent with the poem's official morality. It is necessary for women to stop shining on all alike. That is dangerously unsettling to society. They must pair-bond, settle down, and begin to cultivate the resources of personality that are summed up in the phrases 'good humour' and 'good sense'. Perhaps it is good advice, but it is also tinged with a corrosive sense that beautiful women were outside the poet's reach, beyond his capacity to attract or possess.

When Pope relaunched himself as an original poet with the publication of the 1728 version of *The Dunciad*, there was a new sense of scale and purpose about his work. A volume of Pope's *Works* had appeared in 1717, marking him out as the leading young writer of the age but also making him an object of widespread dislike. Pope kept an elaborate scrapbook of such attacks, suggesting that he was always intending to settle scores, but it was Lewis Theobald's *Shakespeare Restored* (1726), an attack on Pope's edition of *Hamlet* running to some 200 pages, that tipped him over the edge. In some respects, the Pope/Theobald quarrel was a reprise of the Dryden/Shadwell stand-off. Just as Dryden has persuaded generations of readers that Shadwell is a dunce, Pope's *Dunciad* gained a lasting victory over Theobald, despite the latter's far superior expertise as an editor of Shakespeare. An even-handed account of Alexander Pope's achievement as editor might conclude that his strengths were intimately bound up in his weaknesses. His finely tuned ear resulted in an ability to correct the aberrant lineations of seventeenth-century texts; and, contrary to some opinions, he did make considerable use of early quarto editions. He was, however, a slave to his own notions of poetic decorum and was frequently insensitive to the pronunciation, metrics, and stylistics of earlier English drama. Seeing scribal and printers' errors where none existed, Pope made very many unnecessary emendations. Much of this was pointed out by Theobald, using only one play as a specimen. Theobald demonstrated over and over again his knowledge of Shakespeare's period, of the early quartos, and of other dramatists writing at the time. This formidable indication of what Theobald might do if he chose led to Pope's retaliation. On the model of a comic version of Homer's *Iliad*, Pope composed *The Dunciad* in three books, with Lewis Theobald as its hero instantiating the epic values. Public demand for *The Dunciad* was so great that it was reissued in 1729 as *The Dunciad Variorum*, a grandiose edition supposedly edited by a mock-learned pedant called Martinus Scriblerus, who buries the text under a byzantine editorial machinery. In the poem, Pope constructs the myth that there is a collective phenomenon called 'Dulness' presided over by a goddess bearing that name, and embodied in individuals called 'Dunces'. They have a collective identity somewhere between a political party, an academic college, and the labourers in a factory for the manufacture of bad writing. They live in identifiable, generally shady and poor, parts of London; but, just as the action of the Homeric epics dramatizes a move westwards from Troy to the foundation of Rome, and just as the barbaric tribes of the dark

41

ages later moved east to west to sack Rome and end civilization, so the Dunces are always going west. Overcrowding their
allotted spaces, they threaten to overrun the polite areas of
London where Court and government have their seats. Behind
this mythology is a metaphysical scheme, part-pagan and
part-Judaeo-Christian, in which civilization is perpetually
threatened by the goddess Dulness's desire to restore the
empire of primal stupidity and mental anarchy over which she
once reigned. The dunces' activities in morale sapping and
intellectual undermining are tools in this project of inverted
Restoration. As in *The Rape of the Lock*, Pope crams into the
narrow compass of three books all the main incidents that one
expects from an epic. Theobald is discovered in Book I
pondering how best to make a living. He summons the
goddess by means of a sacrificial burning of his works and is
transported by her to the Temple of Dulness, where he is
anointed king. The coronation is celebrated in Book II by heroic
games in which booksellers and critics contend for appropriate
prizes. Events include a booksellers' race, a pissing contest, a
muck-raking treasure hunt on the bed of the sewer, and finally
a test for the critics, to see how long they can resist sleep when
the works of two authors are read aloud. In Book III, the King,
slumbering in the Goddess's lap, is transported to the Elysian
shades, where, under the guidance of a minor poet, he is
shown visions of the past and future triumphs of Dulness and
is privileged to witness the prophecy of the arts and sciences
being overrun by a new anarchic barbarism.

The Dunciad takes much further the attack on proliferating
print that we noticed in embryo in *An Essay on Criticism*, an
aspect that we will investigate further in later discussions. For
the present, we concentrate on the poem as an attack on
popular culture. Theobald was involved in writing scripts for
pantomimes, a new art form well described by Thomas Wilkes
in his *A General View of the Stage* (1759):

> Harlequin is generally supposed to be some being under the
> power of enchantment, in love with, and beloved by, Colombine;
> but crossed in all his designs by Pantaloon her father, his man
> Pierrot, and the Squire who courts her. Harlequin's only wit
> consists in his activity, displayed in escaping from them either by

assuming another form, turning a bed-chamber into a garden, a tavern into a church, or hunting his pursuers with spirits. After a number of pursuits, crossings, turnings, and transformations, some god or superior being interposes in favour of the enchanter Harlequin, makes him friends with his pursuers, and gives him Colombine for a wife.[4]

In *The Dunciad*, pantomime and opera combine in a two-pronged attack on sensible forms of culture and entertainment. Meaningless because silent (pantomime) or sung in Italian (opera), those two forms create a toy shop of special effects, brainless spectacle, and supernatural quackery lacking in moral or intellectual value. Having worked for the theatrical impresario John Rich in the 1720s to develop the synthesis of opera, ballet, spectacle, acrobatics, and farce that is early pantomime, Lewis Theobald was now setting himself up as a serious editor of Shakespeare in opposition to Pope himself! The culminating vision of the 1728/9 *Dunciad* occurs when Theobald, like Moses, Aeneas, and Adam before him (in *Paradise Lost*), is taken by the ghost of a hack writer, Elkanah Settle, to a Mount of Vision and is shown the shape of things to come. He sees, but fails to recognize, a 'sable Sorc'rer' who is his own Harlequin Dr Faustus, creating the special effects from his own pantomime of 1725, *Harlequin a Sorceror, with the Lives of Pluto and Proserpine*, represented by Pope as a comic transformation of the Creation. Pantomime is uncreation, antimatter, an alternative universe 'to Nature's laws unknown':

> He look'd, and saw a sable Sorc'rer rise,
> Swift to whose hand a winged volume flies:
> All sudden, Gorgons hiss, and Dragons glare,
> And ten-horn'd fiends and Giants rush to war.
> Hell rises, Heav'n descends, and dance on Earth,
> Gods, imps, and monsters, music, rage, and mirth,
> A fire, a jig, a battle and a ball,
> Till one wide Conflagration swallows all.
> Thence a new World, to Nature's laws unknown,
> Breaks out refulgent, with a heav'n its own:
> Another Cynthia her new journey runs,
> And other planets circle other suns:
> The forests dance, the rivers upward rise,
> Whales sport in woods, and dolphins in the skies,

And last, to give the whole creation grace,
Lo! one vast Egg produces human race.
   Joy fills his soul, joy innocent of thought:
'What pow'r,' he cries, 'what pow'r these wonders wrought?'
'Son! what thou seek'st is in thee. Look, and find
Each monster meets its likeness in thy mind.

(P. 416, III. 229–48)

Theobald's amnesiac state is such that he cannot recognize the
phantoms of his own brain. Scenic effects create a Book of
Revelation vision of the end of the world, followed by
Harlequin's frequently depicted birth out of a giant egg, a
perversely oviparous alternative to normal parturition. This is
a fitting emblem of the topsy-turvy universe of pantomime,
one that breaches all natural laws. The passage culminates in
a wonderful moment of self-recognition, as Theobald is encouraged to see himself as the god-creator of this chaotic
alternative universe.

Prophetic poetry always attracted Pope. Two pre-1715
poems incorporate resounding prophecies, *Windsor-Forest*
modelled on Virgil's fourth *Georgic*, and *Messiah*. This latter
poem has a Virgilian source, the *Pollio*, but in it Pope tried to
imitate the tones of the prophet Isaiah, in line with a
developing taste for the Hebrew poetry that lies behind the
Authorized Version (1611) of the Old Testament. *Messiah*
culminates in a vision of the coming of Christ, and the
dissolution of this world in a blaze of light:

See Heav'n its sparkling Portals wide display,
And break upon thee in a Flood of Day!
No more the rising *Sun* shall gild the Morn,
Nor evening *Cynthia* fill her silver Horn,
But lost, dissolv'd in thy superior Rays;
One Tyde of Glory, one unclouded Blaze,
O'erflow thy Courts: The LIGHT HIMSELF shall shine
Reveal'd; and *God's* eternal Day be thine!

(P. 194, ll. 97–104)

When he came to write the first *Dunciad* more than a decade
later, he revisited this prophetic mode, but turned it into the
second coming of Anarchy. Again, Pope incorporates both
Judaeo-Christian and classical Greek mythemes in his eclectic

account of uncreation. All the main symbols of plenitude in *Messiah* are turned into negatives, as the Divine injunction 'Let there be light' is countermanded by the goddess of Dulness:

> She comes! the Cloud-compelling Pow'r, behold!
> With Night Primaeval, and with Chaos old.
> Lo! the great Anarch's ancient reign restor'd,
> Light dies before her uncreating word:
> As one by one, at dread Medaea's strain,
> The sick'ning Stars fade off th'aethereal plain;
> As Argus' eyes, by Hermes' wand opprest,
> Clos'd one by one to everlasting rest:
> Thus at her felt approach, and secret might,
> Art after Art goes out, and all is Night.
>
> (P. 424–5, III. 337–46)

The Dunciad is the climactic work in a series of remarkable satires by Pope and his close friends Jonathan Swift and John Gay all written between 1726 and 1729, the best known of which is Swift's *Gulliver's Travels*. The impetus behind this effloration is primarily political, as the next chapter will show; for the present, the minor poems that Pope wrote in reaction to *Gulliver's Travels* will provide a good opportunity to consider the nature of his wit. An aspect of Pope's writing that is only recently coming to be appreciated is the concern he had for the female subject. Several of his most successful early poems – *Eloisa to Abelard*, *Sappho to Phaon*, 'On the Statue of Cleopatra, made into a Fountain by Leo the Tenth' – are written from the female perspective, imagining what it is like to be an abandoned woman, separated from her lover, a voice crying in the wilderness lamenting the emptiness and isolation of her predicament. The fourth of Pope's 'Gulliver' poems, 'Mary Gulliver to Captain Lemuel Gulliver', is a comic version of those earlier poems of pathos. Those who know the novel know that Lemuel Gulliver has returned from his fourth voyage a changed man. He cannot endure the company of humans, especially not his wife and family, preferring those equine companions who bear the closest resemblance to Houyhnhnms. His wife writes an 'expostulating, soothing, and tenderly-complaining Epistle' to her husband, in which she reads her husband's story as an autobiography. She is the most

45

extraordinary reader of the text, both the best and the worst, the most intimately concerned and the most gullible. Naive, literal-minded, inextricably involved, she describes her reactions to the book's main incidents:

> When folks might see thee all the Country round
> For Six-pence, I'd have giv'n a thousand Pound.
> Lord! when the *Giant-Babe* that Head of thine
> Got in his Mouth, my Heart was up in mine!
> When in the *Marrow-Bone* I see thee ramm'd;
> Or on the House-top by the *Monkey* cramm'd;
> The Piteous Images renew my Pain,
> And all thy Dangers I weep o'er again!
> But on the Maiden's *Nipple* when you rid,
> Pray Heav'n, 'twas all a wanton Maiden did!
>
> (P. 488, ll. 79–88)

Pope wittily refers to an obscene crux in *Gulliver's Travels*, where Swift implies that the giant women in Brobdingnag have used Gulliver as a dildo. That is a question in which his wife can be presumed to have an interest! Inventing a wife for Gulliver is an ingenious way of extending Swift's own ontological play with the fictionality of his *Travels*. At the end, Mary's desire to enter into her husband's fantasies by developing the voice of a Houyhnhnm, alluding as it does to the incantatory voices of Quakers and other nonconformist preachers, is both poignant and hilarious:

> Nay, wou'd kind *Jove* my Organs so dispose,
> To hymn harmonious *Houyhnhnm* thro' the Nose,
> I'd call thee *Houyhnhnm*, that high-sounding Name,
> Thy Children's Noses all should twang the same.
> So might I find my loving Spouse of course
> Endu'd with all the *Virtues* of a *Horse*.
>
> (P. 488, ll. 105–10)

Pope's next project seems a very long way away from such *jeux d'esprit* as his Gulliver poems, and yet it is not. From 1726, the man who was to become Pope's 'guide, philosopher, and friend', Henry St John, Lord Bolingbroke, settled at Dawley Farm in Middlesex, where he was a relatively close neighbour of Pope's at Twickenham. Dawley became a cell of organized political opposition to the Whig stranglehold over government exerted by Sir Robert Walpole. Bolingbroke cultivated the view, already strongly seeded in the minds of such writers as Pope, Swift, John Gay, and Henry Fielding, that Walpole offered his financial support only to third-rate writers of the kind attacked by Pope in *The Dunciad*. Afraid of quality, Walpole nourished only hacks and party-writers. Departing from the Roman traditions even of absolute rulers like Emperor Augustus, and from the practice of earlier English monarchs, the Hanoverian kings and their chief minister suppressed independent imagination and creativity, fearing that those who were talented enough to write well were talented enough to see through them. Bolingbroke's dream was to turn the first-rate writers into the cultural arm of his anti-Whig political campaign. In a series of historical essays and in the journalism published in the *Craftsman*, Bolingbroke elaborated an ideology to the effect that English politics was no longer split along party lines into Whigs and Tories. Rather, it was split into a corrupt Court and ministerial clique, and a patriotic opposition of the incorruptible that would find nationwide support amongst the virtuous irrespective of whether those people considered themselves Hanoverian Whigs or Jacobite Tories. 'Patriots' avoided extremes; they were moderates. They put their country's good before their own personal advantage. Acting in concert, prompted by uncompromisable virtue, they were capable of regenerating a one-nation, 'country' spirit that would triumph over the 'party spirit' of the Walpolean Whigs.

Pope's writings in the 1730s take on many elements of this political analysis, even if he became progressively disenchanted with it as the decade wore on and the expected victories did not materialize. It was Bolingbroke who persuaded him that he was capable of producing a massive 'Opus magnum', a great work of philosophical poetry that would enshrine in verse Bolingbroke's own most deeply pondered thoughts about human nature and society as expressed in his philosophical *Fragments*, and possibly in a prose treatise now lost that Pope may actually have been consulting while writing the *Essay on Man*. Pope saw the *Essay* as a general map, a large-scale chart dealing with the 'Nature and State of Man', and the series of *Moral Essays* that preceded and interspersed the *Essay*'s publication as a set of close-up investigations on how people use material possessions, illustrating the general theories of the *Essay*. By 1733, before any part of the *Essay* was published and again under Bolingbroke's prompting, Pope had already commenced his series of *Imitations of Horace* that would turn his life into an exemplary one. Horace, the Roman poet active in the first century BCE, had a career that Pope could have seen as a model for his own. Not born to a noble family, son of a freedman (Pope's father was a linen draper), Horace presents himself as brought up in the traditional Italian style. Several passages in Pope's *Imitations* stress the domestic idyll of his own relatively rusticated upbringing. Horace found his hopes coming to nothing with Brutus' defeat by Mark Antony – for Pope, the fall of the Tory ministry dominated by Bolingbroke on the death of Queen Anne in 1714 might have seemed to be a parallel tragedy. Under Virgil's tutelage, Horace was recommended to the powerful patron Maecenas, then gathering around him a circle of influential writers. Having flirted with Walpolean patronage, Pope adopted Bolingbroke as his Maecenas and, in his letters, refers to him under that name. Horace's security was guaranteed by Maecenas' gift of the Sabine farm in 38 BCE, granting him the leisure to write poetry and ensuring a constant flow of the rich and the opinion-formers to enjoy his hospitality. Pope's garden at Twickenham was cultivated quite consciously on this model. Pope aspired to *be* Horace in his life and his art, except that, whereas Horace had freedom of expression, Pope stressed his own comparative daring and lack of liberty.

With the *Essay* we need not be extensively concerned, because it does not set out to be a satirical work. It does come into the category of poem, however, that is frequently sabotaged by satire. Bolingbrokean in its claims to moderate anti-extremism, as expressed in the aspiration to 'steer betwixt the extremes of doctrine seemingly opposite', actually the *Essay* is not a moderate poem. Pope's problem is that, having set out to 'vindicate the ways of God to Man', he finds that actually he does not *like* human nature very much, and it is difficult not to find God responsible for that at some level! The first epistle is designed to persuade us that, although we cannot apprehend it, the Universe does have an overall design into which we fit. Yet it seems uneconomical for God to have made such a purblind, foolish species, only to work for its benefit behind the scenes. Why not make a more adequate order of being in the first place? Although the account given of mankind at the beginning of the second epistle does conform to the 'middle way' prescription – man is midway between a beast and an angel – Pope's terse, pointed, and brilliant portrait is a dark one:

> Plac'd on this isthmus of a middle state,
> A being darkly wise, and rudely great:
> With too much knowledge for the Sceptic side,
> With too much weakness for the Stoic's pride,
> He hangs between; in doubt to act, or rest,
> In doubt to deem himself a God, or Beast;
> In doubt his Mind or Body to prefer,
> Born but to die, and reas'ning but to err;
> Alike in ignorance, his reason such,
> Whether he thinks too little, or too much;
> Chaos of Thought and Passion, all confus'd;
> Still by himself abus'd, or disabus'd;
> Created half to rise, and half to fall;
> Great lord of all things, yet a prey to all;
> Sole judge of Truth, in endless Error hurl'd:
> The glory, jest, and riddle of the world!
>
> (P. 516, II. 3–18)

Although Pope tries very hard to make sense of human beings as creatures impelled by self-love (what we might perhaps term the survival instinct), the urges of which are controlled by rationality, he never convinces himself or us. How exactly do creatures described as being in the grip of a dominating 'passion' work together for the good of the entire species, as Pope's later epistles assure us that they do? How can 'Self-love and Social be the same'? In the fourth epistle, the circle that Pope has to square is that, while there must be differentiation of rank – 'ORDER is Heav'n's first law' – this does not determine human happiness or fulfilment. The poor and disadvantaged can be just as happy, the poem maintains, as the rich and famous. As a general proposition one doubts this: happiness is a function of opportunity and the ability to satisfy needs. Such an argument is one of the reasons why Pope's *Essay* is sometimes regarded as the expression of vacuous optimism that Voltaire satirized in *Candide*. I find Pope's poem far more troubled and self-divided than complacent, however. Pope's attempt, for example, to reconcile rank with social justice takes him into satiric diatribes against fame that fail to convince. 'What's Fame? a fancy'd life in others breath, | A thing beyond us, ev'n before our death.' Actually, it was something that Pope craved, and that this poem works hard to secure.

The standard library edition of Pope's complete poems, the Twickenham Edition, does not print the poems in the order of publication; it hives off into separate volumes what are called the *Epistles to Several Persons* and the *Imitations of Horace*. The poems appear to be more systematic than they actually were, and the tumbling, somewhat chaotic fecundity of Pope's achievement in the 1730s is not quite apparent to the reader. There is little sense of the drama and controversy that the publication of these poems individually provoked in Pope's lifetime. There are three verse letters written to influential noblemen (Lords Burlington, Bathurst, and Cobham), the aim of which is to explore the doctrine of the 'ruling passion' being elaborated for the *Essay on Man* – the idea that each personality is determined by the dominant influence of a particular trait; to consider how riches can be used and abused; and to explore the relationship that the wealthy man should set up with the natural environment being shaped around him. This last objective is that of the *Epistle to Burlington*, published in December 1731. Burlington was a noble patron of the arts, spearhead of the early century 'Palladian' revival in the style of his villa at Chiswick House. Having made the Grand Tour of Italy to observe Roman architecture, especially that of Vitruvius and Andrea Palladio's reconstructions of it in the sixteenth-century villas he built in northern Italy, Burlington built his own villa to function as a temple of the arts and a shrine of hospitality and conversation. Like Pope's Twickenham and Bolingbroke's Dawley Farm, Chiswick was also a gathering place for the talented, disaffected writers and artists of Hanoverian England. Pope's *Epistle* is an extended compliment to Burlington's taste, his harmonious relationship with his surroundings expressed in an instinctive understanding of the 'Genius of the Place', by which Pope means its spirit or special atmosphere; and the poem includes a portrait of the antithesis to Chiswick, a garish, overblown, gigantic house that he calls 'Timon's Villa':

> At Timon's Villa let us pass a day,
> Where all cry out, 'What sums are thrown away!'
> So proud, so grand, of that stupendous air,
> Soft and Agreeable come never there.
> Greatness, with Timon, dwells in such a draught
> As brings all Brobdingnag before your thought.
> To compass this, his building is a Town,
> His pond an Ocean, his parterre a Down:
> Who but must laugh, the Master when he sees,
> A puny insect, shiv'ring at a breeze!
> Lo, what huge heaps of littleness around!
> The whole, a labour'd Quarry above ground.
> Two Cupids squirt before: a Lake behind
> Improves the keenness of the Northern wind.
> His Gardens next your admiration call,
> On ev'ry side you look, behold the Wall!
> No pleasing Intricacies intervene,
> No artful wildness to perplex the scene;
> Grove nods at grove, each Alley has a brother,
> And half the platform just reflects the other.
> The suff'ring eye inverted Nature sees,
> Trees cut to Statues, Statues thick as trees,
> With here a Fountain, never to be play'd,
> And there a Summer-house, that knows no shade;
> Here Amphitrite sails thro' myrtle bow'rs;
> There Gladiators fight, or die, in flow'rs;
> Un-water'd see the drooping sea-horse mourn,
> And swallows roost in Nilus' dusty Urn.
> My Lord advances with majestic mien,
> Smit with the mighty pleasure, to be seen:
> But soft – by regular approach – not yet-
> First thro' the length of yon hot Terrace sweat,
> And when up ten steep slopes you've dragg'd your thighs,
> Just at his Study-door he'll bless your eyes.
> His Study! with what Authors is it stor'd?
> In Books, not Authors, curious is my Lord . . .

> (P. 592–3, ll. 99–134)

The point is initially one of scale. The villa's owner is entirely out of scale with the house. He looks like Gulliver in the land of the giants. Far from, as he hopes, the house aggrandising him, it reduces him to pitiful insignificance. Nature and art both combine to make the place uncomfortable. Timon has difficulty with his water features! The pond at the rear of the house is so large that it serves simply to augment the cold wind, while the verb 'squirt' used of his two cupid fountains conjures up an image of the statues weakly pissing. For Pope, one of the pioneers of the picturesque movement in landscape gardening, aesthetic taste was defined in terms of harmonious management of contraries – 'artful wildness', 'pleasing intricacies'. Managing planting to combine thick growth with unexpected prospects and views was crucial. Timon's villa is planted in mathematical regularity, wonderfully imitated by the line 'Grove nods at grove, each Alley has a brother', where the medial pause creates the sense of boringly predictable symmetry. The only view you get is the view of the wall. Timon clearly has not discovered one of the great eighteenth-century landscaping innovations, the ha-ha or sunken fence, that creates boundaries between spaces without interrupting the view. For Pope, topiary or ornamental hedging was an example of an entirely wrong-headed relationship between art and nature. Cutting nature into monstrous shapes, especially flowers into military formations, was a sacrilege. The final couplet in the first paragraph is powerfully effective in imaging nature out of its element, but at the same time beginning to recolonize human artefacts as the swallows take over a dry ornamental urn.

When our host emerges to meet his guest, Pope exploits the technical capabilities of the couplet with special brilliance, the pauses mimetic of the length of time it takes actually to reach the main entrance door, and the heavily stressed monosyllabics of 'when up ten steep slopes' rendering the effort of ascending the stairs more like mountain climbing. (We are reminded of Pope's tiny stature and of the physical effort it took for him to dress in the morning. His limbs had to be encased in several layers of linen before he felt warm enough to face the day.) Once inside the house, we learn that it is entirely non-functional, an ornamental show house that creates the most acute discomfort for those who try to live in it. Timon is an aristocratic dunce, who keeps his books to show their fine bindings. As we learn just after the passage quoted, there is no Locke or Milton in his library, because he professes to be too cultured and snooty to collect such modern ephemera! There follows a passage on religious worship *chez* Timon. His chapel is a monument to sensuality, with its fashionable music and semi-pornographic ceiling frescos – no fit place to remind the worshipper of spiritual mysteries. Dinner is a parody of hospitality, the menu being less important than the rituals of service; and, despite the lavish provision, a spirit of penny-pinching meanness actually prevails.

All the four moral essays contain sharp portraits such as this one. The *Epistle to Bathurst*, for instance, published in January 1733, is an attack on all those who stockpile wealth for its own sake and do not redistribute it in for the general good. It culminates in a portrait of a character called 'Balaam', a Protestant nonconformist, whose career in amassing wealth and paying off his conscience is examined from Pope's Catholic perspective. 'Balaam' satirizes the biblical names that puritans were fond of bestowing upon themselves, but is also the name of a venal prophet who was willing to sell his prophecies to the enemies of Israel, as described in the Book of Numbers. Credit, paper money, invisible wealth – a system that enables such as Balaam to trade on their reputations for honesty – is one of the targets of this portrait, as it was for the political opposition to the Whigs who considered that financial paladins, money-men who did not have the same stake in the nation as older landed families, were the conduits of national corruption. The accommodation made between religious principles and commercial values is in Pope's sights here. There is not space to do full justice to the *Epistles to Several Persons*, though we will return to the last of them, the *Epistle to a Lady*, published in February 1735. What needs to be pointed out for the present is the way in which Pope interspersed these letters to the rich and fashionable with imitations of the poet Horace, one aim of which was to counterpoint such satiric portraits with a mythologized account of the poet's own life. Here, in complete contrast with the Timon's Villa portrait, is one of 'Pope at home', that emphasizes the homegrown, English, very domestic quality of the poet's hospitality, from the *Imit. Hor. Sat.* II.ii:

Content with little, I can piddle here
On Broccoli and mutton, round the year;
But ancient friends, (tho' poor, or out of play)
That touch my Bell, I cannot turn away.
'Tis true, no Turbots dignify my boards,
But gudgeons, flounders, what my Thames affords.
To Hounslow-heath I point, and Bansted-down,
Thence comes your mutton, and these chicks my own:
From yon old wallnut-tree a show'r shall fall;
And grapes, long-lingring on my only wall,
And figs, from standard and Espalier join:
The dev'l is in you if you cannot dine.
Then chearful healths (your Mistress shall have place)
And, what's more rare, a Poet shall say *Grace*.

(P. 623, ll. 137–50)

Moderation, spontaneity, the ability to create a delicious meal from ingredients all to hand, a liberalism of atmosphere necessary to permit enjoyment – and yet, controlled by Pope's reference to saying grace. Pope is no Rochester – no godless epicure. As the *Imitations of Horace* rolled off the press, Pope built up a recognizable poetic personality, a persona that serves to guarantee his right to satirize the age, to speak out boldly against vice and political corruption. In *Imit. Hor. Ep.* II.ii. 51–71, he gives us the 'facts' of his upbringing: not university educated, but knowing the difference between right and wrong and suffering persecution for his Catholic affiliations. In the first of his imitations to be published, *Satire* II.i. (February 1733), Pope publishes a manifesto for satire, under-propped by his initial claim that he is an honest, plain-dealing moderate, unaffiliated to any party. Since Bolingbrokean politics were based on an abolition of party, this might not be as innocent as it seems:

My Head and Heart thus flowing thro' my Quill,
Verse-man or Prose-man, term me which you will,
Papist or Protestant, or both between,
Like good *Erasmus* in an honest Mean,
In Moderation placing all my Glory,
While Tories call me Whig, and Whigs a Tory.

(P. 615, ll. 63–8)

If we accept this picture of the entirely scrutable, transparent character as the true Pope, we will be inclined to accept it when, later in the poem, Pope steps up the rhetorical tone:

> Yes, while I live, no rich or noble knave
> Shall walk the World, in credit, to his grave.
> To VIRTUE ONLY and HER FRIENDS, A FRIEND
> The World beside may murmur, or commend.
> Know, all the distant Din that World can keep
> Rolls o'er my *Grotto*, and but sooths my Sleep.
> There, my Retreat the best Companions grace,
> Chiefs, out of War, and Statesmen, out of Place.
> There, *St John* mingles with my friendly Bowl,
> The Feast of Reason and the Flow of Soul . . .
>
> (P. 617, ll. 119–28)

In this and in later imitations, Pope is to present the satirist as a public servant whose art is required in a time of national emergency. Beyond the power of the Church, without recourse to the law, corrupted at source by a poisonous government, the nation has the satirist as its only resource. The satirist is an ultimate deterrent, his shaming ability able to reach corners of society that other agencies cannot. As in the passage above, Pope strikes, then at once retires to his Twickenham fastness, where those, like Henry St John, Lord Bolingbroke, who have been treated shabbily by the nation can gather their strength, leaving the cares of the world far behind them. Pope's most famous gardening feature, the underground passage or 'grotto' he created at Twickenham, is a safe subterranean haven for such men.

Despite the ingeniousness of the Horatian imitations – and this can be appreciated only by comparing Pope's English words to those of Horace's original Latin, as Pope's first readers were encouraged to do by the printing of parallel texts – the finest poems written by Pope in the 1730s were not actually Horatian imitations. The *Epistle to Arbuthnot* published in early 1735, and two dialogue poems called *One Thousand Seven Hundred and Thirty Eight*, sometimes now referred to as the *Epilogue to the Satires: Dialogues I and II* (1738), are not copies of specific poems by Horace, but are infused by the Horatian spirit. Pope's verse letter to Dr John Arbuthnot was written in response to a satirical attack on the poet by his arch-enemies Lady Mary Wortley Montagu and Lord Hervey that aspersed his lowly birth; and in dialogue with John Arbuthnot, physician, polymath, and lifelong friend of the poet. Arbuthnot had requested that Pope keep his satire more general and stop naming identifiable individuals. Pope's poem is an *apologia pro vita sua* that explains and defends his writing by showing that it is a natural consequence of the way in which he has lived his life. It brings Pope's art to perfection, combining the achievements of verse letter and the imitation, mythologizing the blameless, and Christian life of the poet, justifying his satire as a crusade against moral evil and illustrating that evil through three structuring character portraits. Atticus (the writer Joseph Addison), Bufo (the rich patron George Bubb Dodington), and Sporus (John, Lord Hervey) were all powerful Whigs, but the basis of Pope's attack is the symbiotic relationship each set up with flatterers and, if one may say, flatterees. Basing his self-projection on the notion of *independence*, Pope asserts above all that he is a self-made man. Impelled, driven to write, he is nevertheless separable from the hacks, dunces, and poetasters by the fact that his writing found favour in the eyes of the nation's leading arbiters of taste. He writes, in other words, because there is an established desire to read what he writes, created by the merits of that writing. Indeed, the poem opens dramatically, with the poet having to take refuge behind locked doors in Twickenham from the demands that he write more, or read the insane lucubration of others.

> Shut, shut the door, good *John!* fatigu'd I said,
> Tye up the knocker, say I'm sick, I'm dead,
> The Dog-star rages! nay, 'tis past all doubt,
> All *Bedlam*, or *Parnassus*, is let out:
> Fire in each eye, and Papers in each hand,
> They rave, recite, and madden round the land.
>
> (P. 597–8, ll. 1–6)

Outside is a plague-ridden world. Parnassus, sacred to the Muses, is now Bedlam – a lunatic asylum. Afraid of contagion, the poet lurks behind closed doors. In the poem that follows, the poet heals himself by representing to his physician his righteous, blameless life, culminating in a sentimental vignette of Pope actually *becoming* a physician, nursing his dying mother:

> Me, let the tender Office long engage
> To rock the Cradle of reposing Age,
> With lenient Arts extend a Mother's breath,
> Make Langour smile, and smooth the Bed of Death,
> Explore the Thought, explain the asking Eye,
> And keep a while one Parent from the sky!
>
> (P. 612, ll. 408–13)

What Pope finesses are the *market* aspects of his poetic career. He does not probe the many respects in which his writing succeeded, because he was an adroit businessman whose acumen for marketing his work was unrivalled in the history of print. He prefers to represent his progress as a kind of levitation act – no visible means of support! And in that, he contrasts himself to all those who have risen by kissing ass and who, like Atticus/Addison, do not have the courage of their convictions to speak out. As for the poet:

> Not Fortune's Worshipper, nor Fashion's Fool,
> Not Lucre's Madman, nor Ambition's Tool,
> Not proud, nor servile, be one Poet's praise
> That, if he pleas'd, he pleas'd by manly ways.
>
> (P. 608, ll. 334–7)

This assertion of masculinity gains power from coming just after a famous passage (ll. 305–33), in which Pope picks out the gender uncertainties of the androgynous John, Lord Hervey, favourite of Queen Caroline, under the name 'Sporus' – one of Emperor Nero's male lovers. Hervey's malign impotence is perfectly figured in Pope's devastating portrait:

> His Wit, all see-saw between *that* and *this*,
> Now high, now low, now Master up, now Miss,
> And he himself one vile Antithesis.
>
> (P. 608, ll. 323–6)

The tones of the disinterested defender of the public good, struck at the end of the *Epistle to Arbuthnot*, are again sounded in two dialogues both published in 1738 and simply called after that year. Again the conversation, this time with an imaginary friend, is on the topic of Pope's satiric practice. The friend asks why Pope does not act more in accord with his own self-interest and self-preservation? This brings out one of Pope's strongest expressions of the corruption of the age. Virtue is in the whore's cart, while Vice is represented as processing through the streets in a 'Triumphal Car', as if in a Lord Mayor's or Coronation pageant, the corrupted country trailing in her wake:

> Lo! at the Wheels of her Triumphal Car,
> Old *England's* Genius, rough with many a Scar,
> Dragg'd in the Dust! his Arms hang idly round,
> His Flag inverted trails along the ground!

(P. 694, ll. 151–5)

Bolingbrokean in spirit, the lines illustrate the theme that St John had been expressing in his journal the *Craftsman* for many years: the national spirit destroyed by the love of gold. In the second poem, the Friend asks why it is that Pope gets so angry in other people's causes? In answer to that, Pope shows his fearlessness by breaking with decorum and employing a simile that is bound to shock and nauseate the reader. Pope claims that speeches made in parliament are passed from mouth to mouth, rather in the way that Westphalian hogs eat truffles, excrete them, and then leave the droppings for the next hog to eat:

> Let Courtly Wits to Wits afford supply,
> As Hog to Hog in Huts of *Westphaly*;
> If one, thro' Nature's Bounty or his Lord's,
> Has what the frugal, dirty soil affords,
> From him the next receives it, thick or thin,
> As pure a Mess almost as it came in;
> The blessed Benefit, not there confin'd,
> Drops to the third, who nuzzles close behind;
> From tail to mouth, they feed, and they carouse;
> The last, full fairly gives it to the *House*.
>   FR. This filthy Simile, this beastly Line,
> Quite turns my Stomach – P. So does Flatt'ry mine.

(P. 700–1, ll. 171–82)

Such a hideously anal conceit of parliamentarians eating each others' excrement directly refers to a sycophantic funeral speech made by Lord Hervey on Queen Caroline's death, and subsequently used by both Henry Fox and his brother Stephen. The latter was reputed to be one of Hervey's homosexual partners, so the simile alludes to homosexual forms of gratification; and, because Hervey and the Foxes were Walpolean Whigs, the passage suggests a connection between Whiggery and buggery. By the end of the poem, satire has become an ultimate deterrent, a nuclear warhead brought into play when all the normal watchdogs of the constitution have been drugged asleep.

An attempt to write another 'state of the nation' poem such as this was aborted in 1740. Pope was getting tired. He did not see Bolingbroke's opposition succeeding, even although a generation of younger politicians were recruited in the later 1730s and brought new blood. His final projects in poetry would be very different. A revision of the three-book *Dunciad* would come out in 1742; in 1743 the entire poem would be reissued with an added, and much longer, fourth book, and with a new hero, the actor-playwright-manager Colley Cibber. This is more suitably examined in the intellectual context established in the next chapter, so discussion is postponed for the present. To end this account of Pope's life and work, I suggest we return to the period December to April 1734–5, when Pope published several items. The first was a poem published as *Sober Advice from Horace, to the Young Gentlemen about Town*, an imitation of Horace's second Sermon. At various times in his life, and despite the lack of plausibility of the posture, Pope represented himself as a rake. In this very odd poem, odd because it is about the sexual habits of the age and because it is presented as having been edited by the eminent classical scholar Richard Bentley, Pope seems to revert back to a Rochesterian mode. The poem conjures up a demi-monde of rakes and whoremongers more suggestive of the 1670s than the 1730s. The 'advice' being given to Pope's cronies is not to pursue married women, but to confine the appetite to young, willing whores:

> When sharp with Hunger, scorn you to be fed,
> Except on *Pea-Chicks*, at the *Bedford-head?*
> Or, when a tight, neat Girl, will serve the Turn,

In errant Pride, continue stiff, and burn? . . .
Give me a willing Nymph! 'tis all I care,
Extremely clean, and tolerably fair . . .

(P. 672, ll. 149–54)

One doubts whether Pope would have known what to do with such a 'willing Nymph', and one wonders why he wrote this poem. Perhaps it is in a similar category to the girls' school pornography written by Philip Larkin.

Women were, it seems, much on Pope's mind in 1735. More enduringly controversial is the *Epistle to a Lady*, addressed to his close friend (some said his wife) Martha Blount and published in the month after the *Epistle to Arbuthnot*, February 1735. Subtitled 'Of the Characters of Women', the poem is part of the 'opus magnum' project in being a companion piece to those other epistles to Burlington, Bathurst, and Cobham that try to define our essential characteristics as a species. Like those other poems, *To a Lady* works with the conception of the 'Ruling Passion', arguing that women have a somewhat attenuated set of them due to their social conditioning. In saying this, he clearly abandons the psychological determinism that seems to hamper his account of male behaviour in the other poems. *To a Lady* is not popular with feminist-inspired readers of the present generation, owing to the 'essentialism' of thinking that women are different enough to require a separate analysis from men, to some of the things that are actually said about women in the poem, and to what is perceived as the patronizing conclusion in which Martha Blount is presented as a 'softer Man', whose virtues are all passively based on self-denial, retirement, and containment. The virtues that Pope sees in Martha Blount are indeed those recommended by Clarissa in *The Rape of the Lock*, and by Pope to Martha's wilder sister Teresa in the poem earlier mentioned: good temper, modesty, obedience, and the like. This is clearly unfashionable in our own time. As far as the other points go, Pope's point about women is that their sphere of activity is socially determined. Since 'a Woman's seen in Private life alone', they have a less extended sphere in which to develop characteristics, and, since they are 'bred to disguise', they almost inevitably resort to two 'Ruling Passions', 'The Love of

Pleasure, and the Love of Sway'. If women are taught to be objects of desire and pleasure, it is not surprising that they will cultivate power over men in order to prolong that object status as long as possible. Surely this analysis of the female predicament in Pope's time is accurate enough? In perceiving that social conditioning rather than any innate conception of 'femaleness' is responsible for this state of affairs, Pope is actually taking the first steps in feminist criticism, understanding that gender is not a biological given.

Appropriate, then, to record that, in his later life, Pope seems to have attracted the attentions of a female stalker only ever known as 'Amica'. From 1737 until just before his death in 1744, this unidentified female fan was writing to him and to her friends, confessing that she had turned her house into something between a shrine and a museum: 'I have indeed plac'd Mr. Pope in every Room in my Apartments.'[5] By then, the wizened, crooked, hunchbacked bard of Twickenham was a household name.

3

The Ancients, the Moderns, and the Scriblerians

From the previous two chapters, it has appeared that the motive forces of satire in this period were sex and politics: male/female relations; pursuing sexual gratification outside marriage and prolonging it inside marriage; party political allegiances; bribery and corruption. In this chapter, a new dynamic is added. The focus is on beliefs and ideas that arose out of the intellectual ferment of the late seventeenth and early eighteenth centuries. An initial point of entry is offered by what is probably the best-known satirical work of the period, Jonathan Swift's *Travels into Several Remote Nations of the World*, more commonly known as *Gulliver's Travels* (1726). Readers of *Gulliver's Travels* frequently find the third part of the book – *A Voyage to Laputa, Balnibarbi, Luggnagg, Glubbdubdrib and Japan* – a particularly uncomfortable experience. It comes across as a ragbag of unconnected adventures, in which Gulliver's own persona seems to dwindle into the thinnest of vehicles for the author's opinions and prejudices. Many readers find the attitude to scientific progress in this section of the *Travels* difficult to understand. In Laputa, where the men are obsessed with musicology and mathematics, they need to be hit on the nose and mouth by 'flappers' carrying bladders filled with dried peas to prevent them from falling into ditches. In Lagado on Balnibarbi there is an academy in which 'projectors' are engaged in extracting sunbeams from cucumbers, in 're-duc[ing] human excrement to its original food', in building houses from the roof downwards, in teaching spiders to spin silk, in sowing chaff and breeding naked sheep; and, memorably, in using a mechanical engine to write books and devising a means of abolishing all words whatsoever. This involves carrying great sacks of objects around – three-dimensional nouns that form the basis of whatever conversation you plan to have that day. Now, this is clearly some kind of a satire on the illustrious gathering of scientists and learned men known as the Royal Society for the Promotion of Natural Knowledge, which received its Royal charter in 1662 and was to achieve numerous scientific breakthroughs, as reported in its *Philosophical Transactions*, in subsequent decades. Most modern commentators would say that the experimenters of the Royal Society were the crucible of modernity, the brains that made the agricultural and industrial revolutions of the eighteenth- and nineteenth centuries possible. Why, then, did Swift regard them as a legitimate target for satirical attack? Why did Swift get it so wrong? Why was he on the wrong side of the argument over scientific progress, seemingly such an anti-Enlightenment figure?

To understand this, I think we need to understand something about the nature of science itself in the period. We might start with medicine. The foundation of modern medicine is often taken to be William Harvey's 1628 *De motu cordis*, the famous work in which he disproves Galen's theory dating back to the second century CE that blood was absorbed into the body and replaced by new blood made in the liver from a substance called 'chyle'. Harvey showed that the heart was a muscle that worked through ventricles expelling blood in systolic contractions, blood that was pushed through arteries in such quantities per hour that it was more than the entire volume of blood in the body. So blood must, therefore, circulate round the body. Based on observation and dissection (of frogs), Harvey's findings do seem modern. But, as Roy Porter points out in his book *The Greatest Benefit to Mankind* (1997), Harvey saw through Aristotle's spectacles. He did not think of the body as primarily a machine, but as activated by 'vital forces'.[1] The heart was for him as for Aristotle not just a muscle but 'the seat of the soul', an organ deputizing for God in the body, the foundation of all life. And there are many examples of what we might call 'unscientific science' in the period. In 1665, the great bubonic plague, first experienced in England in 1348, returned to London – caused, we now think, by a bacillus transferred to humans by fleas from infected rats, but of course entirely mysterious to the mystified and terrorized citizens of seventeenth-century London. People still believed that the King's touch might cure the plague, and mainly attributed its effects to the wrath of God. A good place to observe this mixed scientific/unscientific attitude to plague is the work of historical fiction published in 1722 by Daniel Defoe, *A Journal of the Plague Year*. This is set during the earlier plague epidemic, narrated by one H.F. who is an eyewitness to the various horrors of the dead carts, mass graves, the exodus from the city, and so on. It is also a scientific work, which presents very powerfully argued views on how such outbreaks should be contained. The practice of shutting up and quarantining houses, for example, was shown to be cruel to the healthy inside and unsuccessful. But within the scientific framework, we get anecdotes like the following:

> I have heard also of some, who in the Death of their Relations, have grown stupid with the insupportable Sorrow, and of one in particular, who was so absolutely overcome with the Pressure upon his Spirits, that by Degrees, his Head sunk into his Body, so between his Shoulders, that the Crown of his Head was very little seen above the Bones of his Shoulders; and by Degrees, loseing both Voice and Sense, his Face looking forward, lay against his Collar-Bone, and cou'd not be kept up any otherwise, unless held up by the Hands of other People.[2]

One cannot quite see this anecdote about the man with the retractable head as scientific, but rather as superstitious and apocryphal. It is very odd to read stories like this in the middle of an otherwise very closely observed and accurate work obsessed with measuring populations, death rates, and the like. Meanwhile in 1665, while the plague was rampaging in London, Isaac Newton was taking refuge in his birth village, Woolsthorpe in Lincolnshire. According to a statement he made about fifty years later (as part of the controversy with Leibniz over the priority for invention of the calculus), this is how he spent his time:

> In the beginning of the year 1665 I found the Method of approximating series & the Rule for reducing any dignity of any

Binomial into such a series. The same year in May I found the method of Tangents of Gregory & Slusius, & in November had the direct method of fluxions & the next year in January had the theory of Colours & in May following I had entrance into the inverse method of fluxions. And the same year I began to think of gravity extending to ye orb of the Moon & from Keplers rule of the perodical times of the Planets being in sesquialterate proportion of their distances from the center of their Orbs, I deduced tht the forces wch keep the Planets in their Orbs must be reciprocally as the squares of their distances from the centers about which they revolve: & thereby compared the force requisite to keep the Moon in her Orb with the force of gravity at the surface of the earth, & found them to answer pretty nearly. All this was in the two plague years of 1665–1666. For in those days I was in the prime of my age for invention & minded Mathematicks and Philosophy more then at any time since.[3]

But the same Newton who could achieve all of this was, within three years of this date, delving deeply into alchemical experiments. His biographer R. S. Westfall shows that, in the 1670s, Newton was part of a clandestine ring of alchemists, that he had in his possession manuscript tracts copied in his own hand, and that those were concerned with the alchemists' age-old quests to make gold and to find the philosopher's stone and the elixirs that would lead to eternal life. So Newton, the founder of modern physics, deviser of the mechanical approach to nature that radically separated mind and matter, was also an alchemist who embraced everything that materialism rejected: nature is life, not machine, all things are generated by the copulation of male and female principles and life forces in nature. Whereas mechanical physics asserted that matter is inert, alchemy deemed that it is imbued with active principles of life and motion. Newton, it seems, was not content with explaining the mysteries of the universe. He needed to put some back!

The point is that the late seventeenth century was a period of dramatic progress in science, philosophy, and learning, an age of optimism in which Newton along with the other great astronomers, physicists, and mathematicians under the auspices of the Royal Society were being credited with explaining the entire universe. But such progress was both uneven and controversial. What was its ultimate aim? Was the aim to pluck God down from his heaven in a Faustian act of overreaching? Were not human beings driven by pride in attempting to prise out all the secrets of creation? What kinds of men were those new scientists? Did they intend to disturb long-established hierarchies of status and knowledge with their new methods? In works like *Gulliver's Travels*, Pope's *Essay on Man* and John Gay's *Fables*, the most salient satirical theme is human *pride.* Working on the assumptions that humankind is made in the image of God and that it is the pinnacle of God's achievement in creation, human beings pride themselves on their knowledge and wisdom. The march of science is a powerful weapon in this campaign to exalt human status. In *Gulliver's Travels*, one of Swift's most subversive tactics is to invent creatures called Houyhnhnms, which to every outward appearance resemble horses, those drudge animals, and call them the 'perfection of nature'. Swift's Houyhnhnms are largely pacifist creatures endowed with a limpid rational faculty, whose approach to life and the mystery of death is entirely matter of fact. Like Friday with Robinson Crusoe, Gulliver at once recognizes the Houyhnhnms, the rational horses, as his natural superiors – much to the fury of readers at the time. It was the endpoint of a process of humbling the reader's pride that goes on throughout the entire work.

In satire by Swift and Pope that precedes and leads up to *Gulliver's Travels* and *The Dunciad*, the great works of the 1720s, the principle target was the pride taken by human beings in the state of current *learning.* It has to be emphasized that there was no hard-and-fast distinction between what we might call 'science' in this era, and what might be called 'humanities'. Scientific methods could also be applied to history and archaeology, reconstituting a more accurate sense of the past. There was a new breed of man, sometimes called a 'virtuoso', dedicated to the application of scientific methods in understanding the past. Such men were viewed with suspicion by the aristocratic guardians of the humane tradition of learning and knowledge. The new breed of virtuoso was devising proto-archaeological methods for learning about ancient civilizations. We cannot just read prestigious works of ancient literature as *examples* to guide modern statesmen and regulators, on the assumption that history goes in cycles and that we can learn directly from the past. Some scholars were realizing that the past is another country. We have to delve into the past, literally to dig it up: we need to study non-prestigious objects like inscriptions on coins or statues, we need to study and display such objects in collections and museums, not just in the libraries of aristocratic country seats. So by the end of the seventeenth century the lines of battle are drawn up between those who think that the new professionalized, scientific scholarship is a threat to powerful aristocrats who have effortlessly possessed the humane learning of the Romans and the Greeks in their families for centuries – the *ancients;* and those who support modern methods of editing, archaeology, and empirical science in the name of intellectual progress – the *moderns.* The earliest skirmishes in this battle were fought in France, over Homer.

Since ancient times, the issue of Homer's identity and poetic achievement had been contested, but in late-seventeenth-century France it became fashionable to think that Virgil was not just a pale Roman imitator of Homer but actually a greater poet in his own right. This argument was taken much further by Charles Perrault, who, between 1688 and 1692, drew up a series of parallels between ancient and modern achievement in the arts, eloquence and drama (*Parallèle entre des anciens et des modernes),* very much in favour of the moderns. Aristotle and Plato achieved nothing comparable to the invention of the telescope; Homer was a great poet but he had the misfortune to live in coarse and brutal times, and his gods were capricious and venal. The Homeric epics, argued Perrault, are punctuated by tedious irrelevant digressions, the most ridiculous of which was that describing Achilles's shield in *Iliad* 18. If it had as many scenes engraved on it as Homer describes, it would be too vast to use! Gradually, Perrault built up the case that the very existence of 'Homer' was doubtful, that the great ancient epics were not single-authored but were assembly jobs, that the story was deficient, the characters badly drawn, the manners of gods and heroes gross, and the whole lacking in refinement and *politesse.* Homer found able defenders in the husband-and-wife team of André and Anne Dacier, the latter of whom was an outstanding Greek scholar who produced a

French prose translation of Homer and, in so doing, defended Homer and his times in scholarly commentaries published in 1711.

Behind the somewhat pointless question of whether the ancients or the moderns were superior was a real and vital issue. What is the true nature of the past, and what kind of historical scholarship is most successful in retrieving it? The 'ancients' insisted on the 'presentness' of the past: classical poetry was applicable to modern life and the work of the ancient historians taught lessons relevant to universal human nature. For the moderns, the main point was that Homer, whoever he was, had written in a world long vanished. The manners and customs of late-seventeenth-century France and England were not those of ancient Greek civilization. A new breed of scholar was emerging – antiquarians and classical philologists who had the equipment necessary to understand the culture and language of ancient Greece. The news they brought back from the front line was alarming to the ancients, those defenders of a gentlemanly, humane way of studying the classics by reading books in the privacy of one's library. Scholars like the German Ludolph Kuster, who produced a synthesis of ancient and modern Homeric scholarship, and the Englishman Joshua Barnes, who published a new complete edition of Homer in 1711, had to go over all the important previous editions and the massive storehouse of commentary from Byzantine to modern times. And they had to consider the archaeological evidence that bore upon classical practices, customs, and beliefs. While Pope was embarking upon his massive couplet edition of Homer between 1715 and 1725, it was becoming more and more apparent that, to be competent as a translator, you had to know about, for example, agricultural methods, burial customs, religious beliefs, forms of political organization, measurement of time, distance and money, military matters, and so forth. The evidence in Pope's case was that he was very far indeed from being a competent Greek scholar. Pope's enemy John Dennis said that he had 'undertaken to translate Homer from Greek of which he does not know one Word, into English, which he understands almost as little'. The business of ransacking the orient for its archaeological treasures had commenced by 1700 – the Earl of

Arundel, for example, had carried off an entire gate from the city of Constantinople – and a steady stream of marbles, manuscripts and coins, inscriptions and busts, was flowing west. To select one or two highlights relevant to Homer, a stone unearthed near Rome carried on it pictorial representations of the Trojan wars, perhaps devised for schoolchildren, known as the *tabulae Iliacae*, which assisted scholars in putting together an account of ancient life. The Frenchman Bernard de Montfaucon published *Antiquité expliquée*, a beautifully illustrated collection of the principal discoveries in antiquarian scholarship to date, including the Iliac tablets. When Pope's translation of the *Iliad* was published in 1720, it sparked off a new episode in the ancients/moderns quarrel because he used his preface and annotation machinery to defend an 'ancient' view of the poet and his achievement, deliberately covering up the elements of scholarship and pedantry that had actually gone into the final product. He defended the feasibility of the Shield of Achilles; and his notes cried up the aesthetic 'beauties' of Homer rather than the textual difficulties it presented.

To understand Jonathan Swift's contribution to this period of intellectual history, we need to go back a little, to the year 1690, just after the ancients/moderns quarrel had broken out in France. In that year, Swift's patron Sir William Temple published an important essay entitled *On Ancient and Modern Learning*, which was to begin the battle between the ancients and the moderns in English intellectual life. Temple was an ancient. He argued that the ancients themselves had access to realms of Egyptian and oriental learning now entirely vanished – and went on to say that there have been no significant intellectual advances since then. The scientists and scholars of the Royal Society could not surpass the ancients in range and extent of knowledge:

> There is nothing new in *Astronomy* to vye with the Ancients, unless it be the *Copernican* System; nor in *Physick*, unless *Hervy*'s Circulation of the blood. But whether either of these be modern discoveries, or derived from old Fountains, is disputed: Nay, it is so, too, whether they are true or no; for though reason may seem to favour them more than the contrary Opinion, yet sense can very hardly allow them; and to satisfie Mankind, both these must concur.[4]

It really seems absurd to deny that Copernicus and Harvey had broken any new ground, and even to suggest that they are not intuitively credible! And Temple went on to make another mistake. In claiming that modern *literature* was as debased as modern science, Temple commended the letters of a supposed ancient Sicilian ruler called Phalaris. Those epistles had been circulating since the Renaissance, but the whiff of forgery always hung over them. And when, in 1695 and 1697, an ancient ally of Temple's called Charles Boyle published a new edition of the letters, the editor and classicist Richard Bentley published a dissertation showing beyond a doubt that they were crude forgeries. Bentley quickly became the object of scathing attacks by a circle of university wits allied to Temple. It is obvious, however, that this was the first major victory for the new 'modern' scholarship. Obviously, too, the basis of the quarrel lay in class or status conflict. The gentleman-amateur Temple, a retired diplomat and member of the landed gentry, saw in ancient learning the ethical values of aristocratic England and felt threatened by the new middle-class profes-sional scholars, whose commitment to advancement seemed to herald a dangerous social mobility. Maybe the entire quarrel would have been forgotten if it had not been for the fact that, when Temple's essay was published, he employed as a secretary on his estate at Moor Park, Surrey, a young man called Jonathan Swift.

Swift published two prose works that are to some extent a contribution to this quarrel. They were certainly written in the 1690s though not published until 1704: *The Battle of the Books* and *A Tale of a Tub*. Now, it would be reasonable to expect that, since Swift was being paid by Temple, those works would be a clear exposition of his views. They would satirize the moderns (specifically, Temple's enemies Bentley and his asso-ciate William Wotton) from an ancient standpoint. But nothing is very straightforward about any aspect of Swift's satirical writing. The *Battle of the Books* is set in the library of St James's Palace, where Bentley worked as the King's librarian. The comic idea is that the 'modern' books in the library want to dispossess the ancient books of their superior shelf space. This leads to an epic battle in which books *become* their authors, and fight it out like epic heroes in *The Iliad*. Bentley is treated like

70

Thersites, an obnoxious, swollen-headed madman, puffed up with self-love and narcissism; and, in the end, he and Wotton are vanquished by Temple and his band of ancients. But Swift's satire, here as everywhere else, seems actually to cut through both sides of the quarrel and has a way of reducing the entire episode to nonsense. As Swift's career advanced, the disconcerting ambivalence of his satiric personae and postures becomes more and more apparent. The opening of the *Battle*, supposedly designed to promote Temple's 'ancient' stand-point, makes this clear:

> Whoever examines with due Circumspection into the *Annual Records* of *Time*, will find it remarked, that *War is the Child of Pride*, and *Pride the Daughter of Riches;* The former of which Assertions may soon be granted; but one cannot so easily subscribe to the latter: For *Pride* is nearly related to Beggary and *Want*, either by Father or Mother, and sometimes by both; And, to speak naturally, it very seldom happens among Men to fall out, when all have enough: Invasions usually travelling from *North* to *South*, that is to say, from Poverty upon Plenty. For . . . we may observe in the Republick of *Dogs* . . . that the whole State is ever in the profoundest Peace, after a full Meal; and, that Civil Broils arise among them, when it happens For one great *Bone* to be seized on by some *leading Dog* . . . The same Reasoning also, holds Place among them, in those Dissensions we behold upon a Turgescency in any of their Females. (S. 1. 141)

This opening abounds in the kinds of pithy moral generaliz-ations that Temple himself liked to make: indeed, there are some direct quotations from him. And it contains some satirical glances at Hobbes's theory of man in a state of nature as being in a state of war ridiculed by Temple also. But Swift's imagery likens both ancients *and* moderns to a pack of hungry dogs pursuing a bitch in heat – surely the effect is to render the whole issue trivial and ignoble. In a later passage, a bee has run into a spider's web in the library, which contest is decided by Aesop in favour of the bee. The spider ventures out to see his web ruined, and the following conversation takes place:

> *A Plague split you,* said he, *for a giddy Son of a Whore; Is it you, with a Vengeance, that have made this Litter here? Could you not look before you, and be d—n'd? Do you think I have nothing else to do (in the Devil's Name) but to Mend and Repair after your Arse? Good Words,*

Friend, said the *Bee* . . . *I'll give you my Hand and Word to come near your Kennel no more; I was never in such a confounded pickle since I was born. Sirrah,* replied the *Spider, if it were not for breaking an old Custom in our Family, never to stir abroad against an Enemy, I should come and teach you better Manners. I pray, have Patience,* said the *Bee, or you will spend your Substance, and for ought I see, you may stand in need of it all, towards the Repair of your House.* (S. 1. 148–9)

It should be clear that the spider represents the modern and the bee the ancient: but the polarities can quite easily be reversed. Although the spider speaks like a rude, unmannerly ignoramus and the bee has all the lightness of touch of a Restoration courtier, what the spider actually *says* makes at least some sense. He accuses the bee of being a vagabond without any personal possessions, who makes a living by 'an universal Plunder upon Nature'; whereas he himself has a 'large Castle . . . all built with my own Hands'. This is how the bee sums up the argument, which is a clear comment on the ancients/moderns dispute:

So that in short, the Question comes all to this: Whether is the nobler Being of the two, That which by a lazy Contemplation of four Inches round; by an overweening Pride, which feeding and engendering on it self, turns all into Excrement and Venom; producing nothing at last but Fly-bane and Cobweb: Or That, which, by an universal Range, with long Search, much Study, true Judgment, and Distinction of Things, brings home Honey and Wax. (S. 1. 150)

A Tale of a Tub, which, alongside the much more approachable *Gulliver's Travels*, is one of the two prose works on which Swift's literary reputation rests, derives from the same decade of intellectual ferment. It cannot be narrowly confined to the ancients/moderns quarrel – it far exceeds those limitations. But, equally, it cannot be understood properly without that background. The work seems to be constructed in two different ways. There is a tale of three brothers, Peter, Martin, and Jack, threading through the whole thing, clearly intended as an allegory of the history of the Christian Church. Peter is a Catholic, Jack an extreme Protestant, and Martin a more moderate Protestant. Ubiquitous in Swift's writing is a technique of literalizing metaphors that, in his hands, has vast comic and satiric potential. The Holy Scriptures might be thought of as a father's will to his children – direct, unambiguous, not to be interpreted against the grain of its root meaning; and the Church, its practices and ornaments, might be thought of as a simple garment or coat – not to be torn, or adorned, or otherwise interfered with against the spirit of its primitive simplicity. The allegorical sections of *A Tale* show how the three brothers all (including to some extent the moderate one, Martin, who presumably represents Swift's own Anglican Church) set out to alter the coat and distort the will; so that, by the end, Peter and Jack are represented as sharing an identical form of madness. Like Fascism and Communism, the reader is made to understand that at the extremes the Catholic and Protestant churches have fanaticism, enthusiasm, and totalitarianism in common.

Alternating with this allegory, though also bleeding into it, is a set of digressions in which a narrator, who several times characterizes himself as a 'modern' and as a hack writer, pursues a set of topics ranging from religious extremism, to systems of philosophical thought, to literary criticism and the state of culture, madness, and its relationship to human happiness, and a whole host of other topics. There is even a digression on digressions! The work has so many introductory and prefatory devices, it takes so long to get going, that the reader senses a satire on bookmaking, authorship, vulgar marketing, and self-advertising. *A Tale of a Tub* is in its physical presentation a satire on the then current state of bookmaking. Its virgin reader is faced with an initial catalogue of treatises by the same author even before he or she has had an opportunity to savour this one. There follows an Apology that seems to be largely but not entirely helpful and straightforward, then a postscript to the Apology commenting on the appearance of a new set of notes that we are assured are 'utterly wrong' (so why include them?) and mystifying the question of authorship. The Dedication to Lord Somers is written by someone posing as a bookseller-publisher who does not, it appears, understand simple Latin and whose methods are identifiably those of the hack, dwelling more lovingly on the physical processes and strategies of writing than is at all comfortable. On the other hand, this dedicator seems to score some good points about the rhetoric of current book dedications and brings off a good compliment. There follows a mysterious statement by the bookseller to the reader further complicating the question of authorship. 'The Epistle Dedicatory to his Royal Highness Prince Posterity' makes the point that Posterity will trouble itself very little over most of the literary productions of the current age: and, in this brief letter, a swarm of ephemeral, venal, pointless writers buzzes into the reader's ken – though the specific names mentioned, Dryden, Nahum Tate, Dennis, Bentley, Rymer, and Wotton, do not actually fit that identikit picture. Those writers are not actually dunces.

It seems that the narrator who is guiding us through the experience of reading the work is a 'modern' and a hack. He is an author of the kind that Pope would later immortalize in *The Dunciad*: a poverty-stricken wretch living in a garret whose involvement with authorship has no more noble motive than a desire to eke out a paltry living:

> The shrewdest Pieces of this Treatise, were conceived in Bed, in a Garret: At other times (for a Reason best known to my self) I thought fit to sharpen my Invention with Hunger; and in general, the whole Work was begun, continued, and ended, under a long Course of Physick, and a great want of Money. (S. 1. 27)

Further, the *Tale* is acutely anxious about the way in which modern bookmaking subverts proper education. Books with indexes, for example, offer a lazy, arsy-versy way of reading. Again, using the metaphor of an index as a 'posterior' enables Swift to set up a whole string of literal, somewhat scatological, analogies for the reading process:

> For, to enter the Palace of Learning at the *great Gate*, requires an Expense of Time and Forms; therefore Men of much Haste and little Ceremony, are content to get in by the *Back-Door*. For, the Arts are all in a *flying* March, and therefore more easily subdued by attacking them in the *Rear*. Thus Physicians discover the State of the whole Body, by consulting only what comes from *Behind*. Thus Men catch Knowledge by throwing their *Wit* on the *Posteriors* of a Book, as Boys do Sparrows with flinging *Salt* upon their *Tails*. Thus Human Life is best understood by the wise man's Rule of

Regarding the End. Thus are the Sciences found, like *Hercules*'s oxen, by *tracing them Backwards.* Thus are *old Sciences* unravelled like *old Stockings,* by beginning at the *Foot.* (S. 1. 91)

When the preface and the tale proper finally get under way, there is a relentless concern with reading strategies: interpretation, allegoresis, the dangers inherent in prying beneath the surface of things, the need to remain superficial, insanity as the consequence of unbalanced reading or interpretation, the respects in which unauthoritative embellishment upon basic and simple tenets can lead to fanaticism. Readers are never permitted to get on with their occupation in peace. They are constantly being reminded that their own activity in interpreting the work is fraught with difficulty and danger.

> It were much to be wisht, and I do here humbly propose for an Experiment, that every Prince in *Christendom* will take seven of the *deepest Scholars* in his Dominions, and shut them up close for *seven* Years in *seven* Chambers, with a Command to write *seven* ample Commentaries on this comprehensive Discourse. I shall venture to affirm, that whatever Difference may be found in their several Conjectures, they will be all, without the least Distortion, manifestly deducible from the Text. (S. 1. 117–18)

The *Tale* brings to our attention one of the most important structural characteristics of the satire of this period – the extent to which it depends on *parody.* The Apology has already alerted the reader to the thread of irony running through the work and to the existence of parodic techniques 'where the author personates the style and manner of other writers who he has a mind to expose'. Simon Dentith has provided a valuable definition of the term 'parody': 'any cultural practice which makes a polemical allusive imitation of another cultural production or practice.'[5] Not the least of the *Tale*'s unsettling features is the sense the reader has that the language being used is language borrowed without acknowledgement, or imitated, from other writers for the purpose of ridiculing what they have said. And this is a pervasive feature, perhaps *the* pervasive feature of the satire that, later in this chapter, will be described as 'Scriblerian'. Before discussing this, however, I will give a final example of how the experience of reading *A Tale* works in practice.

The narrator is, as we have said, a hack writer, part of the explosion of the scribbling classes that elsewhere in his writing Swift condemns as requiring to be controlled if not terminated. The narrator is also a 'modern': his inflated pride, the frequent smugness and narcissism of his style, the pride he takes in the intellectual achievements of the present day at the expense of those ancients upon whom, for such as Swift, our stock of knowledge must be based, identifies him as such. He is also something of a fanatic, a contriver of empty philosophical systems and schemes of arid, pointless learning that we should distrust. Section VIII, for instance, begins thus:

> The Learned *Aeolists* maintain the Original Cause of all Things to be *Wind*, from which Principle this whole Universe was at first produced, and into which it must at last be resolved; that the same Breath which had kindled, and blew *up* the Flame of Nature, should one Day blow it *out*. (S. 1. 95)

This is dangerously close to a blasphemous parody of religion itself, because God's breath, his Divine 'inspiration' (etymologically, blowing in), is the force behind all life. In the next section (IX), the narrator tells us that this philosophy of Aeolism was conceived by a madman, the main reason for his madness being the rising upwards from the bowels of foul vapours (an internal farting mechanism!) that condense into rain and irrigate the imagination. This cues us into a section on the pervasiveness and usefulness of insanity. All great philosophers are spoken of as single-minded, fascistic systematizers who want to impose their own ideas on the rest of mankind. Madness is the cause of this desire, madness that in turn is given various ludicrous mechanical causes. Throughout the section, intermingled with the absurdly reductive physical explanations for things, are grains of common sense and statements that the reader might take to be truths. Tempting though it is to dismiss the narrator as one of the madmen he is describing, it is never quite possible to do so. So that, as we read through the section, being assured by the narrator that this vapour-induced madness has been 'the parent of all those mighty revolutions that have happened in *empire*, in *philosophy*, and in *religion*', we are perhaps inclined to dismiss him as a crackpot. But then the following passage occurs:

For, the Brain, in its natural Position and State of Serenity, disposeth its Owner to pass his Life in the common Forms, without any Thought of subduing Multitudes to his own *Power,* his *Reasons,* or his *Visions;* and the more he shapes his Understanding by the Pattern of Human Learning, the less he is inclined to form Parties after his particular Notions . . . But when a Man's Fancy gets *astride* on his Reason, when Imagination is at cuffs with the Senses, and common Understanding, as well as common Sense, is Kickt out of Doors, the first Proselyte he makes, is Himself, and when that is once compass'd, the Difficulty is not so great in bringing over others; A strong Delusion always operating from *without,* as vigorously as from *within* . . . For, if we take an Examination of what is generally understood by *Happiness* . . . we shall find . . . that, *it is a perpetual Possession of being well Deceived.* And first . . . 'tis manifest, what mighty Advantages Fiction has over Truth . . . because Imagination can build nobler Scenes, and produce more wonderful Revolutions than Fortune or Nature will be at Expence to furnish. Nor is Mankind so much to blame in his Choice . . . if we consider that the Debate meerly lies between *Things past,* and *Things conceived;* and so the Question is only this; Whether Things that have Place in the *Imagination,* may not as properly be said to *Exist,* as those that are seated in the *Memory.* (S. 1. 108)

The first part of this does actually seem to be quite a convincing account of the single-minded paranoia that enters the soul of dictators, religious evangelists, and other power-hungry demagogues. It does seem convincing, psychologically, to argue that such people frequently make converts of themselves – that they are entirely sincere and serious about their own rightness. Their strengths and weaknesses are bound up in not recognizing others as equivalent in 'selfhood' to themselves. Can we really endorse a definition of happiness, however, to the effect that it is 'a perpetual possession of being well-deceived'? One assumes that to be deceived is not a good thing, and that whatever happiness is to be gained from it is a fool's paradise. Is fiction more valuable than truth? Not on any orthodox account of morality. What to make of the idea that the products of the imagination are as real as those of the memory? We normally ascribe to remembered events an ontological certainty that simply cannot be given to events that have not yet happened. Yet poets, prophets, seers, and creative people have often entertained the possibility that the imagination has more to offer than the memory. So, however, have the insane. In the final sentences of this paragraph (not quoted) and in the next paragraph, the narrator dismisses all forms of rationality that involve penetrating beneath surfaces. Superficiality is recommended to us as the most valuable condition of being. All analytical forms of thought, all 'depth models', are rejected. And yet the examples given in support of his superficialism by the narrator are surely ironic: 'Last Week I saw a Woman *flay'd*, and you will hardly believe, how much it altered her Person for the worse' (S. 1. 109). 'Well, actually,' says the reader, 'I have no difficulty at all in believing how much it altered her "person" for the worse. And anyway, where exactly did you see this? Was she alive or dead?' All the main images used in the passage – of unmasking, flaying, dissecting – have been traditionally associated with the art of the satirist. So is the passage a coded attack on satire by a narrator whose own commitment to surfaces is itself being satirized? As so often in Swift's work, the author doesn't believe what his narrator is saying; but he doesn't *not* believe it either.

All the important satire of the period 1715–50 has parody as its central mechanism. Writers interested in parody discuss the question whether parody is a radical or a conservative form. Does it undermine forms of cultural and political authority, or does it set out to police and strengthen such forms? At this historical juncture, there is no doubt that the greatest satirical parodists are conservative. Writers like Swift, Pope, John Gay – and, though they would not respond to exactly the same analysis, Henry Fielding and Samuel Johnson – perceived their function as to patrol the boundaries of acceptable and unacceptable cultural practice and production. They saw themselves as holding the line, retreating to older forms of commitment when faced with the tidal wave of ignorance and proliferating print that characterized the current age. As has been partially analysed in discussing Pope's career, this group of writers saw in the Whig ascendancy a wicked collaboration of bad politics and bad art that was associated with the regrettable tendencies emphasized in this chapter: unthinking 'modernism', hack writing, pointless pedantry, fanatical religion, obsessive collecting of worthless artefacts, and dilution of traditional generic forms. In the fourth book that Pope added to his *Dunciad* in 1743, he finds that the entirety of modern education is dumbed down and trivialized. And common to all their writing is a facility for deploying debased genres and forms of expression critically against those who use them uncritically: parody. Pope, Swift, Fielding, and Gay borrowed and used the creative energies of those dunces that they wanted to stigmatize.

Eighteenth-century satire entered a new phase of development when, in October 1713, Swift and the young Alexander Pope, who had recently arrived in London, decided to assemble a group of talented wits and writers to form a satirical club. They enlisted the services of Dr John Arbuthnot, who was personal physician to Queen Anne – antiquarian, mathematician, FRS, FRCS, and the author of a devastating series of political pamphlets called the John Bull pamphlets. Pope brought in the genial and talented John Gay, whose reputation as a playwright and poet was developing; and the fifth member was the Irish poet Thomas Parnell. The idea was to invent a persona that they could use to ridicule the entire gamut of contemporary learning – pedantic editors, critics, philosophers, antiquarians, travellers, hack writers. He was to have the pompous latinized name of Martinus Scriblerus – 'Martin the Scribbler' – and, like the character of Mr Spectator invented by Addison for his highly successful periodical, he would be given a character and a biography. Spoof works would be published in his name, and the reading public would be further confused by Scriblerus *claiming* to be the author of works that other people had written that the Scriblerians thought ridiculous. Although the life of this club was very short – they held regular meetings between October 1713 and July 1714 in Arbuthnot's rooms in St James's Palace – the 'Scriblerians' sowed the seed corn for satirical works and habits of satirical expression that endured for the next thirty years. It revived in spirit whenever the Scriblerians were reunited, as they were in 1715–16 and in 1726–9. Martin's 'autobiography', the *Memoirs of Martinus Scriblerus*, were not published until Pope finally got them together in 1741, when three of the Scriblerians were dead and Swift was on the point of being certified insane, but by then many other important satirical works had been produced in the Scriblerian manner.

The first direct result of the Scriblerian collaboration was a hilarious play written by Pope, Gay, and Arbuthnot and performed in January 1717, called *Three Hours after Marriage*. Its protagonist was Dr Fossile, a thinly disguised version of Dr John Woodward. Woodward was a good example of the best and worst tendencies in the day's science and scholarship. He held advanced views on geology and founded the science of palaeontology (fossils) that contributed so much to the theory of evolution. Yet this 'virtuoso' was also responsible for much that was freakish and absurd. Mountains, he thought, were formed as a result of stones dissolving in the Biblical Flood and precipitating out after it stopped raining. He held murderous medical views, believing that disorders of the bile caused most human disease. As a result he prescribed courses of laxatives and vomits to his unhappy patients, many of whom did not survive his treatment. Despite being an excellent archaeologist, he was duped by a forged sixteenth-century German candle-holder, which he thought was a genuine Roman antiquity, a shield. The Scriblerians targeted him because he embodied the arrogance and prideful self-assurance of the new science. In the play, he is an Egyptologist awaiting the arrival of two curiosities for his museum – a mummy and a crocodile. To beget an heir, he has just married a young wife, Mrs Townley, who, as her name suggests, is up to speed with all the tricks of the town and is intriguing with two actors, Plotwell and Underplot, who are attempting to cuckold the superannuated old wreck on his very nuptial day. They gain admission to her boudoir disguised as the mummy and the crocodile. Fossile is represented as being so obsessed, so unworldly, so much on the side of death rather than life, so much preferring rust to lust, that he deserves his fate. The play's secondary target is the world of hack writing. Fossile's niece, Phoebe Clinket, is a half-crazed playwright, whose play is set in the time of Noah's Flood and dramatizes some of Fossile's ideas on dissolving stones, and who is willing to be seduced by a self-important critic called Sir Tremendous in order to get her play staged. Sir Tremendous is none other than John Dennis, the critic who had been Pope's sworn enemy since the *Essay on Criticism* ridiculed his use of the epithet 'tremendous'.

Taking up from Swift's analysis of hack writing in *A Tale of a Tub*, Scriblerian satire regards the scribbling mentality as symptomatic of pervasive moral decline. Authors ought to be the custodians of a nation's moral values, but dilettante writers like Phoebe Clinket are emblematic of a widespread cultural malaise. Creative writing should be an expression of the spirit. The hack who writes primarily to gain a living, sitting in his tumbledown garret beset by his bodily needs, is turning airy inspiration into lead. Under the pseudonym Martinus Scriblerus, Pope brought out a little treatise in 1728 called *Peri Bathous; or, The Art of Sinking in Poetry*. Parodying the influential Renaissance work *On the Sublime in Poetry*, *The Art of Sinking* advises would-be writers to avoid poetry's capacity to transcend ordinary language, and opt instead for bathos. Rather than inspiration being the creative breath that allows poets to ascend like the lark, poets should infuse their souls with lead. They should sink into the mud, their inspiration turned into halitosis. They should plumb depths, fall instead of rise, sink instead of swim. In chapter 5, Pope turns his attention to our old friend Sir Richard Blackmore, the poet of the new Age of Lead. Analysing his metaphors for God in his various epic poems, Pope shows how they all succeed in diminishing rather than exalting God's stature and are all therefore examples of bathos:

> But to convince you that nothing is so great which a marvellous genius, prompted by this laudable zeal, is not able to lessen; hear how the most sublime of all Beings is represented in the following images,
> First he is a PAINTER.
> > *Sometimes the Lord of Nature in the air,*
> > *Spreads forth his clouds, his sable canvas, where*
> > *His pencil, dipp'd in heavenly colour bright,*
> > *Paints his fair rain-bow, charming to the sight.*

And in subsequent metaphorical extracts, Pope finds God presented as a chemist, a wrestler, a recruiting officer, a 'peaceable guarantee', an attorney, a gold-beater, a fuller, a 'mercer, or packer', a butler, and, finally, a baker:

> > *God in the wilderness his table spread,*
> > *And in his airy Ovens bak'd their bread.*

> (*B*. 194–5)

The great satirical masterpieces of the period 1726–30 are all 'Scriblerian' in inspiration. All use parodic techniques, where they as it were 'paste up' specimens of hack writing and lowbrow art for polemical purposes, to expose them as ludicrous and unintelligent: but all transcend this parodic intention in creating entirely independent and original works. I have argued elsewhere, and will only briefly recap here, the view that Swift's *Gulliver's Travels* partly responds to a climate in which early novelists like John Dunton, Delarivier Manley, Daniel Defoe, and Eliza Haywood were picking up the kind of storytelling pioneered by seventeenth-century French romance-writers, by travel writers, crime writers, and others, and transposing it into compelling narratives aimed at new markets.[6] For Swift, the claims to truth and seriousness being made by such writers as Defoe were exaggerated and absurd and they are parodied in the claims made by the supposed author of the *Travels*, Lemuel Gulliver, in the 'Letter to his Cousin Sympson'. In the body of the work, the *Travels* is at times itself a parody-romance – for example, in the first voyage to Lilliput, when Gulliver's intrigues with a six-inch-high court lady briefly capture the attention. Gulliver is at other times a parody-Crusoe, who, instead of becoming master to a servant from an indigenous culture, becomes servant to a speaking horse! We have seen that, in *The Dunciad*, Pope targets pantomime, on the one hand, and opera, on the other, as art forms that, in defying all laws of realism and probability, are exemplary of the decay of taste and judgement in audiences. To make the point, though, Pope has to render accurately what those art forms can do. Perhaps the pinnacle of achievement in parodic satirical art is achieved by John Gay in the play that was the most successful in the entire century, premiered in January 1728, *The Beggar's Opera*.

Opera as we know it came to England first in 1705, when Sir John Vanbrugh opened a new theatre, Queen's Haymarket, dedicated to the art of Italian opera. Vanbrugh thought he saw a gap in the market. Aristocrats who had been to Italy and France were passionate about the opera. It was entirely sung throughout – no dialogue, unlike the so-called semi-operas that were already a part of the English entertainment scene – and was sung in the Italian language. Classical history and legend supplied the plots. This kind of thing had never been fully accepted in England, however. From the beginning, there was thought to be something profoundly contrary to the roast beefy spirit of old England in all this emasculated foreign stuff. Immediately after opera's debut in England, the critic John Dennis wrote an *Essay on the Operas* in which he says:

> Musick may be made profitable as well as delightful, if it is subordinate to some nobler Art and subservient to Reason; but if it presumes not only to degenerate from its antient Severity, from its sacred Solemnity, but to set up for it self, and to grow independent, as it does in our late Operas, it becomes a mere sensual Delight, utterly incapable of informing the Understanding, or reforming the Will; and for that very reason utterly unfit to be made a publick Diversion; and then the more charming it grows, it becomes more pernicious.[7]

In his influential *Spectator* papers, Joseph Addison attacked the artificiality of its conventions, in particular the silliness of recitative. *Spectator* 29:

> There is nothing that has more startled our *English* Audience, than the *Italian Recitativo* at its first entrance upon the Stage. People were wonderfully surprised to hear Generals singing the Word of Command, and Ladies delivering Messages in Musick. Our Country-men could not forbear laughing when they heard a Lover chanting out a Billet-doux, and even the Superscription of a Letter set to a Tune. The Famous Blunder in an old play of *Enter a King alone and two Fidlers* was no longer an Absurdity, when it was impossible for a Hero in a Desart or a Princess in her Closet, to speak anything unaccompanied with Musical Instruments.[8]

Those early attacks by Dennis and Addison were followed by many more. Opera was accused of being unintelligible, effeminate, addicting its audiences to luxury and thus emasculating them, destructive of rational, legitimate theatre, and so on. By the 1720s, opera was quite socially divisive. In 1719, a group of noblemen had formed the Royal Academy of Music to give opera the financial backing it required and, hopefully, to make huge profits by promoting this new public taste. Handel was appointed its Musical Director, and he was sent off to Europe on talent-spotting exercises. He brought back the castrato Senesino, and two sopranos, Francesca Cuzzoni and Faustina

Bordoni; but the extraordinarily narcissistic moodiness of these superstars was to lead to trouble. In 1727, the two soprano *prime donne* broke into a hair-pulling, cheek-scratching catfight during a performance of Bononcini's *Astianette*. This was the cultural situation into which John Gay's *Beggar's Opera* intervened when it was staged in January 1728, and became the most successful theatre piece of the century.

Gay wanted to create a low-life, all-English version of Italian opera. From the titles of the songs he used – 'All in the Downs', 'Have you heard of a frolicsome ditty', 'Irish trot', 'Good morrow, gossip Joan', and 'Irish howl' – it is clear that Gay did not go, for the sources of his music, to high art. He found his songs in contemporary popular songbooks, and they included folk songs, traditional old favourites like Greensleeves, love songs, dance tunes, the occasional political propaganda song like 'Lilliburlero' (which was an anti-Catholic song written in the late seventeenth century) or the Jacobite song 'Bonnie Dundee'. He even very cheekily stole the clothes of Italian opera itself. At the beginning of Act II, the highwaymen sing a rousing chorus from Handel's *Rinaldo*, but they turn it into a song about going on the road and robbing purses. It is not just the kind of music, though: it is the entirely new way in which music *interacts* with dialogue that is distinctive about *The Beggar's Opera*. Because it is relatively simple music requiring little in the way of orchestration, there does not need to be a long, statuesque pause while the singer gets ready to deliver the aria. Music can arise as if spontaneously from dramatic situation. It can interact flexibly with lyrics. And here, Gay's play could claim to be the prototype of all modern music theatre, leading to, for example, the kind of *songspiel* that Bertolt Brecht and Kurt Weill produced in the 1930s, and even perhaps Broadway musicals.

In discussing *The Dunciad*, I tried to show how the poem begins in parody of the ancient epic but uses the energy of the dunces to create a new artwork – a kind of tragicomic epic. I think *The Beggar's Opera* can be described in a similar way. Like *The Dunciad*, it has its roots in real life. The character of Peachum was based on a real-life gangster of the period, Jonathan Wild. While in jail for debt, Wild had contracted a liaison with a prostitute and pickpocket, a real-life Moll

84

Flanders, called Mary Milliner. They were partners until Wild cut off one of her ears in a quarrel! Together they set up a business that involved payrolling a gang of thieves and highwaymen to steal, receiving the goods they stole, and then selling those goods back to their rightful owners. In this way, Wild gained the power of life and death over those in the gang because he could always impeach them for the reward, and he also gained a respectable reputation as a friend to the public. Along with the city marshall, Charles Hitchen, Wild developed a sideline in apprehending disorderly persons unless they would pay protection money. What Gay picked up on in all of this was the veneer of respectability. Peachum in the play regards himself as an entirely respectable man of business, using the latest methods of double-entry bookkeeping and arrogating to himself the tones and postures of a substantial merchant. His 'wife' develops the idiom of the ornamental, suburban helpmeet of this considerable burgher; and they are anxious that their daughter Polly should rise in the world. And this introduces a series of paradoxes that structure the entire experience of the play. Whoring becomes more respectable than marriage. Highwaymen are in some respects better men than politicians and urban professionals such as lawyers and preachers. Peachum's indignation is expressed in song in Act I, Scene ix, at the fact that lawyers are even bigger cheats than he aspires to be: while a fox might steal your poultry and a thief your goods, if anyone hires a lawyer, 'he steals your whole estate'. And it is in this way that Gay manages to slip into the performance a cultural analysis that is not unlike that of Alexander Pope's *Dunciad*.

We have seen that, in the mid-1720s, there was a cultural opposition forming against the stranglehold that Sir Robert Walpole increasingly maintained over government and its propaganda machine. In *Gulliver's Travels* and *The Dunciad* there are shadowy representations of Walpole, and there are too in *The Beggar's Opera*. The relationship between Peachum and Lockit carries some of the freight here. Directly, this takes its impetus from Jonathan Wild's partnership with Hitchen. But throughout there are a series of suggested parallels between the criminal gang and the equivalent criminal gang that is currently running the country. The ubiquity of money,

85

the domination of 'business' interests and accounting mentalities, is seen to be the sinister solvent into which all morality is melting. Peachum's relationship with Lockit is suggestive of Walpole's with his brother-in-law Townshend; and the state of mutually assured destruction in which they live reflects on government. And yet, there are allusions to the Brutus/Cassius quarrel in *Julius Caesar* in the quarrel scene, so that the dimension of literary parody is never entirely neglected.

But there is clearly something in *The Beggar's Opera* that goes beyond contemporary political or literary satire. In the twentieth century particularly, after the rise of socialism, the play proved to be a magnet for writers who wanted to apply its basic situations to an analysis of their own times. Bertolt Brecht's *The Threepenny Opera* is, of course, the most famous, but in 1975 the sometime Czech dissident who was later to be President of the Czech Republic, Václav Havel, produced a loose version of the play in the Czech language, which was ruthlessly suppressed by the Czech government and secret police. An English translation by Paul Wilson appeared in 2001. Nick Dear's *The Villains' Opera* was staged at the National Theatre in 2000 – set in gangland London, dominated by drug dealing and bent coppers. Dear is also taken by Gay's 'world-turned-upside-down' analysis of the criminal class, being in some respects less corrupt, or at least more honestly corrupt, than those who supposedly uphold the law and the government.

The spectacular success of *The Beggar's Opera* in the 1727–8 season had a formative influence on the early career of Henry Fielding, whose first decade as a creative writer was devoted to writing and producing plays. Ideologically close to the Scriblerians, Fielding accepted much of their analysis: a prostituted literary world overrun with scribblers and shoddy publishers; a political world dominated by corruption using its patronage to promote only second-rate writers. Like the Scriblerians, Fielding deployed parodic devices to get his points across. In the theatre, the ideal parodic form was the rehearsal play. This format had been devised in 1671 by George Villiers, 2nd Duke of Buckingham, who used it brilliantly in a play called *The Rehearsal* to satirize John Dryden. Since Restoration satire has also been our concern in this book, it is not a digression to spend a little time on *The Rehearsal* before we see what later comic satirists did with it.

Buckingham's motives for producing the play show the same combination of the political and the aesthetic that we have seen going hand in hand throughout this study. Dryden was a Royalist who supported King Charles II even when it became clear that he had deserted his Protestant allies, was doing secret deals with Louis XIV of France, and had a brother who was openly Catholic. Buckingham was in the process of deserting the King over those issues. Dryden was a powerful and charismatic writer, a thorough professional who drew the hostility of aristocratic amateurs like Buckingham, who resented the social mobility that the latter's talents conferred upon him. Further, Dryden was producing plays that were difficult to understand on current generic rules. His tragedies such as *Tyrannick Love* (1669) and the two-part *The Conquest of Granada* (1670) were written on such a scale that ordinary mortals found it difficult to relate to them. Heroes like Maximin and Almanzor hailed from a sealed-off epic universe in which, using a rhetorically inflated idiom festooned with figurative elaboration, they contemplated poker faced their love-versus-honour dilemmas. As well as heroic tragedies, Dryden was writing collaborative semi-operatic tragicomedies such as *The Indian Queen* and an all-singing, all-dancing adaptation of *The Tempest*, which again seemed unintelligible from traditional generic standpoints. So, in *The Rehearsal*, the dramatist Bayes (an easily recognizable portrait of Dryden, who had just been appointed Poet Laureate) is rehearsing a new play and has invited two men of sense, Smith and Johnson, to come along. Smith and Johnson play 'good cop/bad cop' with Bayes, Smith asking blunt, confrontational questions that expose the idiocy of Bayes's dramaturgy, while Johnson collaborates with Bayes, frequently offering far-fetched justifications for his ludicrous practices in order to draw Bayes further into them. Instead of setting his play in the Moghul Empire, Morocco, or some suitably exotic location, Bayes's play takes place in Brentford. After a bullying prologue from 'thunder and lightning', two Kings of Brentford are introduced, only to be summarily usurped by their Usher and Physician. What follows is like a film with bad continuity.

Characters are introduced without the audience having any idea who they are, they whisper for long periods, or make decisions never communicated to the audience; there are dances and songs at entirely inappropriate points in the action. A typical passage of action occurs after the usurpation, depicted by having the Usher and Physician sit on two great chairs then march out flourishing their swords. A character enters called Shirly, whose function is to give us the sense that the world is in turmoil by saying:

> Hey ho, hey ho: what a change is here! Hey day,
> hey day! I know not what to do, nor what to say.[9]

Eight men then enter from two separate doors, exchange lines about friendship, kill each other – and music then strikes up. On a particular musical note, the corpses have been instructed to resurrect, but they have such difficulty in resurrecting to the music chosen by Bayes that he demonstrates – only to fall flat on his face and break his nose. To Smith, Bayes says, 'Pray, Sir, can you help me to a wet piece of brown paper?' Smith replies, 'No indeed, Sir; I don't usually carry any about me'. Throughout the rehearsal, Bayes is represented as a dandified French fop whose language is so metaphorically decorated as to be frequently unintelligible. He is a money-grubbing professional writer, whose love of novelty and brainless spectacle belies his hypocritical rhetoric of the gentleman-amateur:

> But Mr. *Johnson*, i' gad, I am not like other persons; they care not what becomes of their things, so they can but get mony for 'em: now, i' gad, when I write, if it be not just as it should be in every circumstance, to every particular, i'gad: I am no more able to endure it, I am not my self, I'm out of my wits, and all that, I'm the strangest person in the whole world. For what care I for mony? I write for Reputation.[10]

In his plays written in the 1730s, Fielding used the rehearsal format to draw attention to the debased state of the contemporary theatre and to the political world outside the theatre that was ultimately responsible for that debasement. Like John Gay, whose writing for the stage implied the criticism that there is no longer any clear distinction between comic theatre and tragic theatre – that everything has been reduced to a kind of tragicomic stew, or to low farce – Fielding wrote plays that deliberately and comically blurred the boundaries between what makes us laugh and what makes us cry. He refunctions earlier plays so as to parody them and satirize their high-faluting aspirations. Ambrose Philips's very successful tragedy from 1712 *The Distrest Mother* becomes his own *The Covent-Garden Tragedy* (1732), which turns Philips's classical Andromache and Hermione into two whores, Kissinda and Stormandra, while the noble Pyrrhus and Orestes become two rakes, Bilkum and Lovegirlo, with the mother herself becoming Mother Punchbowl, an alcohol-soaked brothel madam. Perhaps his most enduring parodic success has been *Tom Thumb the Great; or The Tragedy of Tragedies* (1730), which, in its published version, has an editorial apparatus similar to that used by Pope in *The Dunciad*, listing passages from over forty plays that were parodied in *Thumb*, making the graphic point that the play was compiled in large measure out of lines of dialogue that other dramatists actually wrote seriously. The play is set in King Arthur's court, to which the six-inch tall conquering hero Tom Thumb has returned in triumph. The King rewards him with the normal-sized Princess Huncamunca's hand in marriage (shades of Gulliver in Lilliput), much to the distress of Queen Dollalolla, herself distracted with love for Thumb. The love-triangle situation is the staple of such plays as Dryden's version of *Antony and Cleopatra* called *All for Love*, and had already been travestied in *The Beggar's Opera.* Dollalolla and the wicked courtier Grizzle conspire to poison Thumb to prevent him from being another's (as Lucy attempts to poison Polly Peachum in *The Beggar's Opera*). There is a tense moment when it is reported that Thumb is dead, but – false alarm – the corpse is only a monkey *resembling* Thumb and dressed in his clothes. The nuptials are about to be solemnized when in bursts the courtier Noodle with the dreadful news that a large cow has swallowed Thumb. Provoked by Thumb's ghost, an orgy of killing and suicide ends the play, resulting in the death of every single character, parodying the pile of corpses to be found at the end of bloody tragedy. Such an ending hits at the debased taste of contemporary audiences while making genuinely comic entertainment out of it.

As Fielding's plays became more overt in their criticism of the Whig regime and of Walpole in particular, as well as more ingenious in their methods of satire, government attempts to suppress him developed in reaction. The passing, in 1737, of the Theatrical Licensing Act shut down the unofficial, fringe venues where his plays were staged. This act of government censorship was a repressive measure that, amongst others, fuelled Alexander Pope's fury in the *Imitations of Horace*, and played its part in his thinking that it was time to bring out a new, improved version of his 'ultimate deterrent', *The Dunciad*.

A concatenation of circumstances led to Pope's decision to publish a new book of verse, *The New Dunciad*, in 1742, and then in 1743 to produce a complete revision of the entire poem in four books, altering the text, the commentary, and the critical apparatus – and, a total surprise to the reading public, presenting a new hero, the playwright-actor-theatre impresario Colley Cibber. Personalities played a vital part. Lewis Theobald, the scholar-hero of the earlier poem, was no longer considered suitable, if indeed he ever had been, to instantiate the poem's mock-epic values. Close to death, Theobald now lacked any significant influence on the cultural scene; and Pope must have known in his bones that Theobald had had the better of their editorial locking of horns. Cibber was, by contrast, an ubiquitous figure, whose publication of his autobiography in 1740, quaintly entitled *An Apology for the Life of Mr Colley Cibber . . . Written by Himself*, was precisely the act of narcissistic exhibitionism that Pope's brass-necked hero would perpetrate, at the same time as being a wonderful source of material for Pope to mine and parody. Cibber was commercial to the soles of his boots, something that his *Apology* did not try to conceal. He saw himself not as a great artist, removed by his talent from the ambit of ordinary men and women, but on the contrary as an entertainer, man of the people, *among* the crowd and *of* the crowd. For Pope, he was the perfect symbol of art-marketed as art-debased, the living proof of the *Dunciad*'s thesis of cultural miscegenation and pollution. Furthermore, in 1742 he published a scurrilous pamphlet, *A Letter from Mr Cibber, To Mr Pope*, in which he gives a graphic and comical description of having rescued the poet, for the sake of his health, *in flagrante* with a prostitute. A combination of the personal and the political, petty vendettas and a much broader set of cultural anxieties, had always been and were again now the motivating forces of Popeian satire. Cibber gives a credibility to the first three books of *The Dunciad* that it lacked with Theobald at the centre, even if some of the lines – for example, those dealing with his library in Book I – are more appropriate to his predecessor. In the new fourth book, however, Cibber is referred to as 'Bays', spends his time in the lap of the goddess Dulness, and plays very little part in the action. This is because the impetus behind the fourth book is really very different from the rest. It refers back to the Scriblerian project and to the ancients/moderns dispute that we have seen to be central to it.

In 1741, Pope finally brought the centrepiece of the old Scriblerus project to fruition by publishing *Memoirs of the Extraordinary Life, Works, and Discoveries of Martinus Scriblerus.* The shadowy figure credited with several earlier treatises and with the commentary and notes for the 1729 *Dunciad* was finally to make himself known. The son of an unreconstructed 'ancient', Martinus is an identikit modern. Virtuoso, philosopher, scientist, his interest in corpses and coins, in rusty old artefacts and modern materialist systems of philosophical thought gives him a kinship with Swift's modern in *A Tale of a Tub*. Dark, brooding, 'generally taken for a decay'd Gentleman of Spain', Martinus is a Don Quixote figure, with a Sancho Panza-like servant Crambe addicted to punning. *Don Quixote* includes throughout a rich vein of slapstick humour, and making Martin a Cervantic type enables Pope to take this element to quite extraordinary lengths. At the basis of Scriblerian satire had always been the tension between body and soul in the human complex, and much of the comedy results from the betrayal of spirit by soma, from the rebellion of physical needs against the dignity of the human spirit. The centrepiece of the *Memoirs* is a chapter parodying romantic fiction, in which Martin falls in love with one of a pair of conjoined twins. He sees Lindamira–Indamora at a freak show (described as if it were some wondrous magical place out of Italian epic) and it is his philosophical curiosity about them that causes him to fall in love with Lindamira. Since the twins have only a single set of genitals, and since the freak-show owner decides to protect his investment by marrying Indamora to one of his other exhibits, the pygmy prince Ebn-Hai-Paw-Waw, the resulting emotional, physiological, and legal tangles are hilarious provided one does not think too deeply about the cruelty of the entire joke. One of the triumphs of the period's mock-heroic humour comes when Martin is eloping with Lindamira (and perforce Indamora), but the pair get stuck in a window sash in a revealing state of undress. This inflames the passions of another of the freak exhibits, a 'Manteger' (a kind of humanized baboon), who attacks Martin. The resulting combat, utilizing all the artefacts from a virtuoso's museum as weapons, is overlaid with allusions to classical literature and the great Homeric epics:

> Lindamira hasten'd to the Alarm of Love, when behold a new Disaster! As she was getting out of the window, the weight of her body on one side, and that of Indamora's on the other, unluckily caused them to stick in the midway: Lindamira hung with her coats stript up to the navel without, and Indamora in no less immodest posture within. The Manteger, who for his gentleness was allowed to walk at large in the house, was so heightened at this sight, that he rushed upon Indamora like a barbarous Ravisher. Indamora cried aloud for help. Martin flew to revenge this insolent attempt of a Rape on his wedding-day. The lustful Monster, driven from our double Lucrece, fled into the middle of the room, pursued by the valorous and indignant Martin. Three times the hot Manteger, frighted at the furious Menaces of his Antagonist, made a circle round the chamber, and three times the swift-footed Martin pursued him. He caught up the *Horn* of a *Unicorn*, which lay ready for the entertainment of the curious spectator, and brandishing it over the his head in airy circles, hurled it against the hairy son of Hanniman [Hanuman, an ape god of India] . . . (*M.* 152)

The Manteger is eventually killed by 'the *hand* of a prodigious *Sea-Monster*', and Martin's victory is celebrated by 'the lady from the window, like another Helen from the Trojan wall', springing from the window ledge and embracing her champion's neck and shoulders with her open legs.

Thinking about Martinus's upbringing at the hands of an obsessed father determined to emulate only the practices of the ancients, editing the various papers that the Scriblerians had left in his possession, Pope turned to the old questions of learning, and in particular of education, that had interested him throughout his creative life. The new fourth book that he added to the *Dunciad* in 1742 was almost entirely on that subject. *Why* had intellectual life become so debased and trivialized in his lifetime? What accounted for the spread of triviality, the dumbing down, the conviction on the part of hack writers that they had something important to tell the world in print? Pope's final analysis of this is that it results from an educational system poisoned at source. Lynchpin sections of Book IV feature a schoolmaster whose mission is to confine schoolboys to a hell of verbal quibbling, where words have become divorced from their referents:

> Then thus. Since Man from beast by Words is known,
> Words are man's province, Words we teach alone.
> When Reason doubtful, like the Samian letter,
> Points him two ways, the narrower is the better.
> Plac'd at the door of Learning, youth to guide,
> We never suffer it to stand too wide.
> To ask, to guess, to know, as they commence,
> As Fancy opens the quick springs of Sense,
> We ply the Memory, we load the brain,
> Bind rebel Wit, and double chain on chain,
> Confine the thought, to exercise the breath;
> And keep them in the pale of Words till death.
>
> (P. 774, iv. 149–60)

University education takes over this anti-creative mission, as the old enemy from the days of the Phalaris controversy in the 1690s, Richard Bentley, is introduced to embody the spirit of Cambridge University:

> For thee [Dulness] we dim the eyes, and stuff the head
> With all such reading as was never read:
> For thee explain a thing till all men doubt it,
> And write about it, Goddess, and about it:
>
> (P. 789, iv. 249–53)

Noblemen on the grand tour, idle bands of virtuosi and collectors, ungodly clergymen lacking humility, dilettanti – a procession of the uneducated and the ineducable make their way to the throne of the goddess to be distinguished by honours and titles at her hands. And the poem ends with the

93

succumbing of the Muse herself to the forces of darkness and chaos. It is an old man's poem, the work of a writer at the end of a highly successful and yet profoundly unsatisfying career, one whose mission to reform the nation through his satire has so clearly failed.

Ironically, Pope's *Dunciad* is nowadays often regarded even by students of the period as virtually unreadable – an example of, not a corrective to, the imprisonment in boredom and verbiage that is its main satirical target. It is in some respects a victim of its own success. As its recent editor, Valerie Rumbold, remarks, 'many features of its appearance testify to [Pope's] aspiration to present it as a modern classic, at the same time as parodying what he saw as the excesses of modern editors'.[11] Much clearer and plainer in its typographical conventions than was typical of eighteenth-century books, it nevertheless does have this vastly complex edifice of prefaces, notes, notes on the notes, and appendices, that makes it almost an early example of hypertext. Reading it is a vertiginous and dizzying experience. It borrows so much energy from the forms of hack and scholarly writing that it parodies, that for the modern reader it is sometimes difficult to distinguish it from them. I hope that this contextual account of its emergence from a particular set of ideas and cultural assumptions, as well as its place in the career of a particular writer, will help readers to value it, and even to enjoy it.

Notes

INTRODUCTION

1. Samuel Butler, *Hudibras*, ed. John Wilders (Oxford, 1967), 797–800; bk. 1, canto 2, ll. 775–88.
2. Jürgen Habermas, *The Structural Transformation of the Public Sphere: An Inquiry into a Category of Bourgeois Society*, trans. Thomas Burger with the assistance of Frederick Lawrence (Cambridge, 1989).
3. *Poems on Affairs of State: Augustan Satirical Verse, 1660–1714*, ed. George de Forest Lord, 7 vols. (New Haven, 1963–75).
4. *Anthology of Poems on Affairs of State: Augustan Satirical Verse, 1660–1714*, ed. George de Forest Lord (New Haven, 1975), 598.

CHAPTER 1. RESTORATION SATIRE

1. John Oldham, *Satyrs upon the Jesuits*, ll. 281–91, 302–3, quoted from *The Poems of John Oldham*, ed. Harold F. Brooks and Raman Selden (Oxford, 1986), 15–16.
2. Oldham, Prologue to *Satyrs*, ll. 26–9, in ibid. 5–6.
3. Andrew Marvell, *The Last Instructions to a Painter*, ll.79–96. Quoted from George de F. Lord (ed.), *Anthology of Poems on Affairs of State: Augustan Satirical Verse, 1660–1714* (New Haven: Yale University Press, 1975), 71.
4. Kevin Sharpe, 'Restoration and Reconstitution: Politics, Society and Culture in the England of Charles II', in Catharine MacLeod and Julia Marciari Alexander (eds.), *Painted Ladies: Women at the Court of Charles II* (London, 2001), 18.
5. Jeremy Collier, *A Short View of the Profaneness and Immorality of the English Stage*, quoted from J. E. Spingarn (ed.), *Critical Essays of the Seventeenth Century*, 3 vols. (Oxford, 1906; repr. 1963), iii. 255–6.

6. *The Works of Sir John Vanbrugh* ed. Bonamy Dobrée, 4 vols (London, 1927), 1.195–96.

CHAPTER 2. ALEXANDER POPE

1. Quoted in Maynard Mack, *Alexander Pope: A Life* (New Haven, 1985), 760.
2. Quoted in ibid. 761.
3. Sir Richard Blackmore, Preface to *Prince Arthur* (London, 1695), unpaginated.
4. Thomas Wilkes, *A General View of the Stage* (London, 1759).
5. Quoted by Mack, *Alexander Pope*, 800.

CHAPTER 3. THE ANCIENTS, THE MODERNS, AND THE SCRIBLERIANS

1. Roy Porter, *The Greatest Benefit to Mankind: A Medical History of Humanity from Antiquity to the Present Day* (London, 1997), 215.
2. Daniel Defoe, *A Journal of the Plague Year* (1722), ed. Louis Landa (Oxford, 1972), 120.
3. Quoted in R. S. Westfall, *Never at Rest: A Biography of Isaac Newton* (Cambridge, 1980), 143.
4. Sir William Temple, *On Ancient and Modern Learning* (1690), quoted from J. E. Spingarn (ed.), *Critical Essays of the Seventeenth Century*, 3 vols. (Oxford, 1906; repr. 1963), iii. 55–6.
5. Simon Dentith, *Parody* (London, 2000), 20.
6. See Brean S. Hammond, *Professional Imaginative Writing in England, 1670–1750* (Oxford, 1997), 271 ff.
7. John Dennis, *An Essay on the Operas after the Italian Manner* (1706), quoted from *The Critical Works of John Dennis*, ed. E. N. Hooker, 2 vols. (Baltimore, 1939), i. 385.
8. Joseph Addison, *The Spectator*, Tuesday, 3 April 1711.
9. George Villiers, Duke of Buckingham, *The Rehearsal*, ed. D. E. L. Crane (Durham, 1976), II. iv. 77–8.
10. Ibid. III. v. 166–74.
11. Valerie Rumbold, 'Introduction', in Alexander Pope, *The Dunciad In Four Books*, ed. Valerie Rumbold (Harlow, 1999), 16.

Select Bibliography

EDITIONS AND BIOGRAPHIES OF MAJOR AUTHORS

Dryden

The Works of John Dryden, ed. Edward Niles Hooker, H. T. Sweden-berg, et al. (Berkeley and Los Angeles: University of California Press, 1955–). 'The California edition' is the main library edition.

The Poems of John Dryden, ed. Paul Hammond and David Hopkins, 4 vols. (Harlow: Longman Annotated English Poems, 1995–2000). Increasingly being seen as the best annotated edition.

Hammond, Paul, *John Dryden: A Literary Life* (Basingstoke; Macmillan, 1991). A very lively brief study.

Winn, James Anderson, *John Dryden and his World* (New Haven: Yale University Press, 1987). The best account of Dryden's life.

Gay

John Gay: Dramatic Works, ed. John Fuller, 2 vols. (Oxford: Clarendon Press, 1983).

John Gay: Poetry and Prose, ed. Vinton Dearing and Charles Beckwith, 2 vols. (Oxford: Clarendon Press, 1974).

Several individual editions of *The Beggar's Opera* are available.

Nokes, David, *John Gay: A Profession of Friendship* (Oxford: Oxford University Press, 1995). The standard biography.

Fielding

The Wesleyan Edition of the Works of Fielding, ed. Marvin Zirker et al. (Lebanon: University Press of New England, 1988–). In progress; the first volume of *Plays* (1728–31) ed. Thomas Lockwood is recently published by OUP.

Joseph Andrews and Shamela, ed. Douglas Brooks-Davies, with a new introduction by Thomas Keymer (World's Classics; Oxford: Oxford University Press, 1999). The best recent edition.

The Beggar's Opera and other Eighteenth-Century Plays, ed. David Lindsay (London: Everyman, 1993). Includes Fielding's *The Tragedy of Tragedies*.

The Regent's Restoration Drama Series published in the 1960s by Edward Arnold has editions of individual plays by Fielding, but they are now out of print.

Battestin, Martin C., and Battestin, Ruth R., *Henry Fielding: A Life* (London: Routledge, 1989). The definitive biography.

Pagliaro, Harold, *Henry Fielding: A Literary Life* (Basingstoke: Macmillan,1998). A shorter alternative.

Rogers, Pat, *Henry Fielding: A Biography* (New York: Scribner, 1979). Preceded Battestin with a short, readable, and good-humoured study.

Pope

The Poems of Alexander Pope, ed. John Butt et al., 11 vols. (London: Methuen, 1938–69). The main reference edition of Pope – usually referred to as the Twickenham Edition.

The Poems of Alexander Pope, ed. John Butt (London: Methuen, 1963 and later reprints). A condensation of the Twickenham edition into a one-volume paperback edition (without Pope's Homer), which I have quoted from in this book.

The Dunciad in Four Books, ed. Valerie Rumbold (Longmans Annotated Poets; Harlow: Longman, 1999).

The Prose Works of Alexander Pope, ed. Norman Ault and Rosemary Cowler, 2 vols. (Oxford: Blackwell, 1936–86). The library edition of Pope's prose.

The Correspondence of Alexander Pope, ed. George Sherburn, 5 vols. (Oxford: Clarendon Press, 1956). Contains most of his letters.

Selected Prose of Alexander Pope, ed. Paul Hammond (Cambridge: Cambridge University Press, 1987). A good selection.

Selected Poetry, ed. Pat Rogers (Oxford: Oxford University Press, 1996). The most available of several selections.

Mack, Maynard, *Alexander Pope: A Life* (New Haven: Yale University Press in association with W. W. Norton, 1985). The definitive biography.

Rosslyn, Felicity, *Alexander Pope: A Literary Life* (Basingstoke: Macmillan, 1990). A much briefer and lively alternative.

Rochester

The Works of John Wilmot, Earl of Rochester, ed. Harold Love (Oxford: Oxford University Press, 1999). The main library edition.

Greene, Graham, *Lord Rochester's Monkey: Being the Life of John Wilmot, Second Earl of Rochester* (London : Bodley Head, 1974). A curious account of Rochester's life in the absence of any authoritative biography.

Swift

The Prose Works of Jonathan Swift, ed. Herbert Davis et al., 14 vols. (Oxford: Basil Blackwell, 1939–68). The main library edition.

Jonathan Swift: The Complete Poems, ed. Pat Rogers (Harmondsworth: Penguin, 1983). The most convenient place to find his complete poems.

Gulliver's Travels, ed. Christopher Fox (Boston: St Martin's Press, 1995). The edition out of very many possibles to be recommended for its critical essays and helpful annotation.

Jonathan Swift, ed. David Woolley and Angus Ross (The Oxford Authors; Oxford: Oxford University Press, 1986). The best compact edition.

The Correspondence of Jonathan Swift, ed. Harold Williams, rev. David Woolley, 5 vols. (Oxford: Clarendon Press, 1963–72). Contains Swift's letters.

Ehrenpreis, Irvin, *Swift: The Man, his Works, and the Age*, 3 vols. (London: Methuen; Cambridge, MA: Harvard University Press, 1962–83). The definitive account of Swift's life.

Glendinning, Victoria, *Jonathan Swift* (London : Hutchinson, 1998). The most sensational biography.

Nokes, David, *Jonathan Swift: A Hypocrite Revers'd* (Oxford: Oxford University Press, 1985). A more radical alternative to Ehrenpreis.

CRITICAL STUDIES OF MAJOR AUTHORS

Dryden

Erskine-Hill, Howard, *Poetry of Opposition and Revolution: Dryden to Wordsworth* (Oxford: Clarendon Press, 1996). Persuasive account of the politics of Dryden's poetry and a compelling portrait, in particular, of the poet's final decade.

Harth, Philip, *Pen for a Party: Dryden's Tory Propaganda in its Contexts* (Princeton: Princeton University Press, 1993).

Hopkins, David, *John Dryden* (Cambridge: Cambridge University Press, 1986). Combines critical comment with a chronological exposition of Dryden's writing career. Consistently able to suggest fruitful approaches to the poet.

99

Miner, Earl, and Brady, Jennifer (eds.), *Literary Transmission and Authority: Dryden and Other Writers* (Cambridge: Cambridge University Press, 1993). Jennifer Brady's essay on Dryden's response to predecessors and interaction with successors is especially interesting here.

Myers, William, *Dryden* (London: Hutchinson, 1973).

Wykes, David, *A Preface to Dryden* (London: Longman, 1977). Lively, well-illustrated, and organized introductory book.

Fielding

Bell, Ian A., *Henry Fielding: Authorship and Authority* (London: Longman, 1994). Breaks new ground in uniting lively analyses of Fielding's work to an awareness of literary theory and to a historicizing approach.

Campbell, Jill, *Natural Masques: Gender and Identity in Fielding's Plays and Novels* (Stanford, Calif.: Stanford University Press, 1995). An exciting book, applying modern gender theory to Fielding's work.

Hume, Robert, *Henry Fielding and the London Theatre, 1728–37* (Oxford: Oxford University Press, 1988). Hume considers that events in theatrical history were more significant than political events in shaping Fielding's career in the theatre. This is a very substantial reassessment.

Lewis, Peter, *Fielding's Burlesque Drama: Its Place in the Tradition* (Edinburgh: Edinburgh University Press, 1987). A useful contextualization of Fielding's dramatic burlesques written in the 1730s against a longer tradition of such meta-theatrical works.

Rawson, Claude, *Henry Fielding and the Augustan Ideal under Stress* (London: Routledge & Kegan Paul, 1972). A collection of separate studies linked by Rawson's ideas of 'disruptive pressures' and 'radical insecurities' in Augustan writing. Typically of this critic, his connections between Fielding and later writers are stimulating.

Gay

Lewis, Peter, and Wood, Nigel (eds.), *John Gay and the Scriblerians* (London: Vision Press, 1988). Essays by Peter Lewis and Pat Rogers deal with *The Beggar's Opera*. Brean Hammond's essay gives an overview of Gay's career.

Winton, Calhoun, *John Gay and the London Theatre* (Louisville: Kentucky University Press, 1993). An uneven book, but it has a very interesting and knowledgeable section on *The Beggar's Opera*.

Pope

Collections

Erskine-Hill, Howard, *Alexander Pope: World and Word* (Oxford: Oxford University Press, 1998).

Fairer, David (ed.), *Pope: New Contexts* (Brighton: Harvester Wheatsheaf, 1990).

Hammond, Brean (ed.), *Pope* (Longman Critical Reader; London: Longman, 1996). A valuable resource.

Mack, Maynard , and Winn, James (eds.), *Pope: Recent Essays by Several Hands* (Brighton: Harvester, 1980).

Nicholson, Colin (eds.), *Alexander Pope: Essays for the Tercentenary* (Aberdeen: Aberdeen University Press, 1988).

Rogers, Pat, *Essays on Pope* (Cambridge: Cambridge University Press, 1993).

Rousseau, G. S., and Rogers, Pat (eds.), *The Enduring Legacy: Alexander Pope Tercentenary Essays* (Cambridge: Cambridge University Press, 1988).

Monographs

Damrosch, Leo, Jr., *The Imaginative World of Alexander Pope* (Berkeley and Los Angeles: University of California Press, 1987). An unpretentious, well-written book that distinguishes clearly between Pope's period and the Restoration and Romantic periods, giving a good account of Pope's experience and ideas.

Deutsch, Helen, *Resemblance and Disgrace: Alexander Pope and the Deformation of Culture* (Cambridge, Mass: Harvard University Press, 1996). Difficult reading but the most successful application to Pope of an approach based on the cultural politics of the body.

Erskine-Hill, Howard, *The Social Milieu of Alexander Pope* (New Haven: Yale University Press, 1985). A pioneering study of the social, political, and economic history of Pope and his circle.

Gordon, Ian, *A Preface to Pope* (London: Longman, 1993). A very well organized introduction, setting Pope in the context of his life, his habitat, the artistic circles he moved in, and the belief system he held. There is a critical survey that gives some readings of key poems.

Hammond, Brean S., *Pope* (Brighton: Harvester Wheatsheaf, 1986). A politicized rereading of Pope that relates the poet's work to its cultural conditions of production.

Mack, Maynard, *The Garden and the City: Retirement and Politics in the Later Poetry of Pope, 1731–43* (Toronto: University of Toronto Press, 1969). Not recent, but one of the most enduring books on Pope, having a masterly grasp of the relationship between the poet, his classical predecessors, and his contemporary friends and allies.

McLaverty, James, *Pope, Print and Meaning* (Oxford: Oxford University Press, 2001). The chapter on *The Dunciad* is amongst the best ever written on the materiality of print and the satirical significance of Pope's use of his medium.

Pollak, Ellen, *The Poetics of Sexual Myth: Gender and Ideology in the Verse of Swift and Pope* (Chicago: University of Chicago Press, 1985). Not entirely free from jargon, but the comparison between Swift and Pope that comes out of this study forms the basis for much subsequent comparative study.

Rogers, Pat, *An Introduction to Pope* (London: Methuen, 1975). One of the best general introductions to Pope available.

Rumbold, Valerie, *Woman's Place in Pope's World* (Cambridge: Cambridge University Press, 1989). How did Pope and his writing figure in the lives of the women about whom he writes? Not a modish feminist book, but one with vast knowledge.

Rochester

Burns, Edward (ed.), *Reading Rochester* (Liverpool: Liverpool University Press, 1995). Paul Baines's essay in this volume considers the relationships between Rochester and Pope.

Fisher, Nicholas (ed.), *That Second Bottle: Essays on John Wilmot, Earl of Rochester* (Manchester: Manchester University Press, 2000). Contains essays on some of Rochester's most important satires, including Brean Hammond and Paulina Kewes's on *A Satyre against Reason and Mankind* as a poem steeped in the contemporary theatre. Julian Ferraro studies Rochester and Pope.

Thormählen, Marianne, *Rochester: The Poems in Context* (Cambridge: Cambridge University Press, 1993). Comprehensive and scholarly account of Rochester's intellectual heritage.

Swift

Elias, A. C., *Swift at Moor Park* (Pennsylvania University Press, 1982). A study of the conditions of composition of *A Tale of a Tub*, and a very able critical reading of it.

Fabricant, Carole, *Swift's Landscape* (Baltimore: Johns Hopkins University Press, 1982). Explains the Irish background to such works as *A Tale of a Tub* and *Gulliver's Travels*.

Phiddian, Robert, *Swift's Parody* (Cambridge: Cambridge University Press, 1995). A superb account of how to apply poststructuralist theories of the text to Swift's early satires.

Rawson, Claude, *God, Gulliver and Genocide* (Oxford: Oxford University Press, 2001). Although the book begins well before the eighteenth century and ends well after it, it includes one of the most compelling and nuanced accounts of *Gulliver's Travels* ever given, by a scholar who has been a major influence on Swift studies.

—— *Gulliver and the Gentle Reader* (London: Routledge & Kegan Paul, 1973). Rawson's historically informed and brilliant close reading of texts, combined with his ability to relate eighteenth-century and modern concerns, makes for heady criticism.

GENERAL

The *Cambridge Companion* series can be recommended in general. The volumes on *English Restoration Theatre* edited by Deborah Payne Fisk, *Eighteenth-Century Poetry* edited by John Sitter, and *English Literature 1650–1740* edited by Stephen Zwicker, are of particular interest to readers of this volume. Blackwells also have *A Companion to Literature from Milton to Blake* ed. David Womersley (Oxford: Basil Blackwell, 2000, repr. 2001), which has sharp readings of most of the major texts covered in this book.

General studies of eighteenth-century writing that provide a valuable understanding of the genre of satire include:

Doody, Margaret, *The Daring Muse: Augustan Poetry Reconsidered* (Cambridge: Cambridge University Press, 1985).

Nokes, David, *Raillery and Rage* (Brighton: Harvester, 1987)

Rothstein, Eric, *Restoration and Eighteenth Century Poetry 1660–1780* (London: Routledge and Kegan Paul, 1981).

Weinbrot, Howard D., *Eighteenth-Century Satire* (Cambridge: Cambridge University Press, 1988).

Studies not specifically about satire, but which provide valuable background to the themes and topics in this book include:

Brewer, John, *The Pleasures of the Imagination: English Culture in the Eighteenth Century* (London: HarperCollins, 1997).

Griffin, Dustin, *Literary Patronage in England, 1660–1800* (Cambridge: Cambridge University Press, 1996).

Hammond, Brean, *Professional Imaginative Writing in England, 1670–1740* (Oxford: Oxford University Press, 1997).

Hughes, Derek, *English Drama, 1660–1700* (Oxford: Oxford University Press, 1996).

Kewes, Paulina, *Authorship and Appropriation: Writing for the Stage in England, 1660–1710* (Oxford: Oxford University Press, 1998).

Langford, Paul, *A Polite and Commercial People: England 1727–1783* (Oxford: Oxford University Press, 1989).

Nicholson, Colin, *Writing and the Rise of Finance* (Cambridge: Cambridge University Press, 1994).

Porter, Roy, *English Society in the Eighteenth Century* (Harmondsworth: Penguin, 1982).

Rawson, Claude, and Mezciems, Jenny (eds.), *The Yearbook of English Studies*, xviii. *Pope, Swift and their Circle* (London: Modern Humanities Research Association, 1988).

Rogers, Pat, *Hacks and Dunces* (London: Methuen, 1980).

Speck, William, *Society and Literature in England 1700–60* (London: Gill & Macmillan, 1983).

Index

Recent and Forthcoming Titles in the New Series of

WRITERS AND THEIR WORK

WRITERS AND THEIR WORK

RECENT & FORTHCOMING TITLES

RECENT & FORTHCOMING TITLES

Title	Author
William Golding 2/e	*Kevin McCarron*
Graham Greene	*Peter Mudford*
Neil M. Gunn	*J. B. Pick*
Ivor Gurney	*John Lucas*
Hamlet 2/e	*Ann Thompson & Neil Taylor*
Thomas Hardy 2/e	*Peter Widdowson*
Tony Harrison	*Joe Kelleher*
William Hazlitt	*J. B. Priestley; R. L. Brett (intro. by Michael Foot)*
Seamus Heaney 2/e	*Andrew Murphy*
George Herbert	*T.S. Eliot (intro. by Peter Porter)*
Geoffrey Hill	*Andrew Roberts*
Gerard Manley Hopkins	*Daniel Brown*
Henrik Ibsen 2/e	*Sally Ledger*
Kazuo Ishiguro 2/e	*Cynthia Wong*
Henry James – The Later Writing	*Barbara Hardy*
James Joyce 2/e	*Steven Connor*
Julius Caesar	*Mary Hamer*
Franz Kafka	*Michael Wood*
John Keats	*Kelvin Everest*
James Kelman	*Gustav Klaus*
Hanif Kureishi	*Ruvani Ranasinha*
Samuel Johnson	*Liz Bellamy*
William Langland: *Piers Plowman*	*Claire Marshall*
King Lear	*Terence Hawkes*
Philip Larkin 2/e	*Laurence Lerner*
D. H. Lawrence	*Linda Ruth Williams*
Doris Lessing	*Elizabeth Maslen*
C. S. Lewis	*William Gray*
Wyndham Lewis and Modernism	*Andrzej Gasiorak*
David Lodge	*Bernard Bergonzi*
Katherine Mansfield	*Andrew Bennett*
Christopher Marlowe	*Thomas Healy*
Andrew Marvell	*Annabel Patterson*
Ian McEwan 2/e	*Kiernan Ryan*
Measure for Measure	*Kate Chedgzoy*
The Merchant of Venice	*Warren Chernaik*
A Midsummer Night's Dream	*Helen Hacket*
Alice Munro	*Ailsa Cox*
Vladimir Nabokov	*Neil Cornwell*
V. S. Naipaul	*Suman Gupta*
Grace Nichols	*Sarah Lawson-Welsh*
Edna O'Brien	*Amanda Greenwood*
Flann O'Brien	*Joe Brooker*
Ben Okri	*Robert Fraser*
George Orwell	*Douglas Kerr*
Othello	*Emma Smith*
Walter Pater	*Laurel Brake*
Brian Patten	*Linda Cookson*
Caryl Phillips	*Helen Thomas*
Harold Pinter	*Mark Batty*
Sylvia Plath 2/e	*Elisabeth Bronfen*
Pope Amongst the Satirists	*Brean Hammond*
Revenge Tragedies of the Renaissance	*Janet Clare*

RECENT & FORTHCOMING TITLES

Title	Author
Jean Rhys 2/e	*Helen Carr*
Richard II	*Margaret Healy*
Richard III	*Edward Burns*
Dorothy Richardson	*Carol Watts*
John Wilmot, Earl of Rochester	*Germaine Greer*
Romeo and Juliet	*Sasha Roberts*
Christina Rossetti	*Kathryn Burlinson*
Salman Rushdie 2/e	*Damian Grant*
Paul Scott	*Jacqueline Banerjee*
The Sensation Novel	*Lyn Pykett*
P. B. Shelley	*Paul Hamilton*
Sir Walter Scott	*Harriet Harvey Wood*
Iain Sinclair	*Robert Sheppard*
Christopher Smart	*Neil Curry*
Wole Soyinka	*Mpalive Msiska*
Muriel Spark	*Brian Cheyette*
Edmund Spenser	*Colin Burrow*
Gertrude Stein	*Nicola Shaughnessy*
Laurence Sterne	*Manfred Pfister*
Bram Stoker	*Andrew Maunder*
Graham Swift	*Peter Widdowson*
Jonathan Swift	*Ian Higgins*
Swinburne	*Catherine Maxwell*
Alfred Tennyson	*Seamus Perry*
W. M. Thackeray	*Richard Salmon*
D. M. Thomas	*Bran Nicol*
J. R. R. Tolkien	*Charles Moseley*
Leo Tolstoy	*John Bayley*
Charles Tomlinson	*Tim Clark*
Anthony Trollope	*Andrew Sanders*
Victorian Quest Romance	*Robert Fraser*
Marina Warner	*Laurence Coupe*
Irvine Welsh	*Berthold Schoene*
Edith Wharton	*Janet Beer*
Oscar Wilde	*Alexandra Warrick*
Angus Wilson	*Peter Conradi*
Mary Wollstonecraft	*Jane Moore*
Women's Gothic 2/e	*E. J. Clery*
Women Poets of the 19th Century	*Emma Mason*
Women Romantic Poets	*Anne Janowitz*
Women Writers of the 17th Century	*Ramona Wray*
Virginia Woolf 2/e	*Laura Marcus*
Working Class Fiction	*Ian Haywood*
W. B. Yeats	*Edward Larrissy*
Charlotte Yonge	*Alethea Hayter*